D0757939

A WAR IT WAS ALWAYS GOING TO LOSE

ALSO BY JEFFREY RECORD

Wanting War: Why the Bush Administration Invaded Iraq

Beating Goliath: Why Insurgencies Win

Dark Victory: America's Second War Against Iraq

*Making War, Thinking History: Munich, Vietnam, and
Presidential Uses of Force from Korea to Kosovo*

Hollow Victory: A Contrary View of the Gulf War

The Wrong War: Why We Lost in Vietnam

Bounding the Global War on Terrorism

RELATED TITLES FROM POTOMAC BOOKS, INC.

Shattered Sword: The Untold Story of the Battle of Midway
—Jonathan Parshall and Anthony Tully

The Pacific War Papers: Japanese Documents of World War II
—Donald M. Goldstein and Katherine V. Dillon, eds.

The Way It Was—Pearl Harbor: The Original Photographs
—J. Michael Wenger, Katherine V. Dillon, and
Donald M. Goldstein

A WAR IT WAS ALWAYS GOING TO LOSE

Why Japan Attacked America in 1941

JEFFREY RECORD

POTOMAC BOOKS, INC.
WASHINGTON, D.C.

Published in the United States by Potomac Books, Inc. All rights reserved. No part of this book may be reproduced in any manner whatsoever without written permission from the publisher, except in the case of brief quotations embodied in critical articles and reviews.

Library of Congress Cataloging-in-Publication Data
Record, Jeffrey.
  A war it was always going to lose : why Japan attacked America in 1941 / Jeffrey Record. — 1st ed.
    p. cm.
  Includes bibliographical references and index.
  ISBN 978-1-59797-534-6 (hardcover : alk. paper)
  1. World War, 1939–1945—Causes. 2. World War, 1939–1945—Japan. 3. Japan—Military policy. 4. Japan—Politics and government—1926–1945. 5. Japan—Foreign relations—United States. 6. United States—Foreign relations—Japan. 7. World War, 1939–1945—Pacific Area. I. Title.
  D742.J3R44 2010
  940.53'110952—dc22

                                                        2010030347

Printed in the United States of America on acid-free paper that meets the American National Standards Institute Z39-48 Standard.

Potomac Books, Inc.
22841 Quicksilver Drive
Dulles, Virginia 20166

First Edition

10 9 8 7 6 5 4 3 2 1

CONTENTS

PREFACE

I was born during the later years of the most destructive war in human history, and I have long been fascinated by its origins. Especially intriguing to me were the folly of Anglo-French appeasement of Hitler, culminating in the sacrifice of democratic Czechoslovakia at the infamous Munich Conference of 1938, and Japan's seemingly suicidal decision, taken in 1941, to attack the United States.

In *The Specter of Munich: Reconsidering the Lessons of Appeasing Hitler,* published by Potomac Books in 2006, I investigated the phenomenon of Anglo-French appeasement and the mythology that has arisen around it, much of it promoted recently by neoconservatives enamored of preventive war. I concluded that nothing short of Hitler's removal from power via assassination, coup d'etat, or foreign invasion could have prevented the outbreak of the Second World War in Europe. The argument of anti-appeasers that Hitler could and should have been deterred from war by firm threats of war by the democracies or by the resurrection of a grand alliance of Great Britain, France, and Russia fails on two counts. First, it ignores Anglo-French military and domestic political realities of the 1930s as well as the prevalent (and at the time) reasonable view that Hitler's ambitions were limited to the rectification of the injustices the democracies had unwisely imposed upon Germany at the Versailles Conference of 1919.

Second, and more important, the deterrence claim ignores the simple fact that Hitler was *inherently undeterrable* because his goals in Europe, which amounted to Germany's subjugation of the entire continent, lay far beyond anything the appeasing states were prepared to accept. Hitler understood that he could not get what he wanted in Europe without war, and therefore was not going to be deterred by the threat of war. War was thus inevitable as long as Hitler remained in power. Only regime change in Berlin could have saved Europe from the calamity of the Second World War, and no one, not even Winston Churchill (at least until 1939), favored Hitler's assassination or an invasion of Germany. Clearly, the appeasers had illusions about Hitler, but no less clearly, as historian Ernest R. May observes, "'Anti-appeasers' had their own illusions which were almost equally distant from reality: They believed that Hitler could be deterred by the threat of war. Few suspected that Hitler *wanted* war."[1] The threat of war cannot be expected to scare off a regime that welcomes war or regards war as inevitable. In this regard, Hitler was fundamentally different from Stalin. Stalin was patient and cautious, his ambitions in Europe were limited, and he responded to credible deterrence.

In the present volume, I examine the road to the Pacific War of 1941–1945 between Japan and the United States, focusing primarily on Japan's decision to attack the United States. The Pacific War arose from Japan's determination to subdue all of East Asia, including resource-rich Southeast Asia, most of which lay under the control of Great Britain, France, the Netherlands, and the United States. Like Nazi Germany, with which it entered into military alliance in 1940, Imperial Japan of the late 1930s and early 1940s was an authoritarian, revisionist power bent on massive territorial conquest at the expense of the democratic West and the Soviet Union. Also like Germany, Japan was undeterrable: Japanese leaders believed that their country's survival as a great power depended on swift imperial expansion, and they were prepared to use force to seize East Asia. By mid-1941 most Japanese leaders had come to regard war with the United States (and Great Britain) as inevitable and a preventive military strike against the United States in the Pacific as imperative.

Yet while Hitler came very close to conquering Europe, including the Soviet Union, the outcome of the Pacific War was never in doubt. Japan was doomed to catastrophic defeat from the moment the first

Japanese bomb landed on Pearl Harbor. Nothing the Japanese could have done—or not have done—after December 7, 1941, would have altered Japan's fate. Japan had no chance against the combination of America's overwhelming material superiority and rage over Pearl Harbor. If there were ever one side that was destined to defeat from the start, it was Japan in the Pacific War.

Why, then, did Japan start that war? Japanese leaders in 1941 were well aware of America's huge superiority in industrial might and latent military power, and all recognized that the American homeland, if not the Philippines and Hawaii, lay beyond Japan's military reach. Most also understood that a fully mobilized United States had the capacity to project enormous military power across the Pacific into East Asian waters, including those surrounding the Japanese home islands; indeed, traditional Japanese naval strategy rested on the assumption that the U.S. Pacific Fleet would come charging across the Pacific to defend the Philippines. Yet against such enormous odds, the Japanese nonetheless opted for war. Why?

CHRONOLOGY OF EVENTS

In U.S.-Japanese Relations, 1931–1941

1931

September   Japan seizes Manchuria.

1932

January   Secretary of State Stimson proclaims U.S. nonrecognition of Manchukuo.

1933

March   Japan withdraws from the League of Nations.

1934

December   Japan declares intention to withdraw from the Washington Naval Treaty of 1922.

1936

August   Japan initiates manpower and industry mobilization for total war.

November   Japan and Germany sign Anti-Comintern Pact.

1937

July   Japan launches wholesale invasion of China.

December   Japanese aircraft bomb and sink USS *Panay* in Yangtze River.

1938

December — Roosevelt approves $25 million loan to Chiang Kai-shek.

1939

February — Japan seizes Hainan Island.

July — United States announces intention to abrogate the 1911 Treaty of Commerce with Japan.

1940

May — Roosevelt orders California-based U.S. Fleet to remain in Hawaii.

June — Japan demands that Vichy regime in Indochina halt flow of supplies to China.

French agree to permit Japanese inspectors in northern Indochina.

Japan announces expansion of New Order in East Asia to "Southern Seas."

July — U.S. Congress passes National Defense Act and Two-Ocean Navy Act.

August — Japan proclaims "Greater East Asia Co-Prosperity Sphere."

September — Japan signs the Tripartite Pact with Germany and Italy.

November — Roosevelt announces $100 million loan to China.

1941

March — First of forty Hull-Nomura meetings begins in Washington, D.C.

May — Roosevelt declares Nationalist China eligible for Lend-Lease.

June — Germany invades Russia; Tokyo considers northward advance into Siberia.

July — Imperial Conference decides on a Japanese advance into Southeast Asia even at the risk of war with the United States and Great Britain.

Japanese forces begin occupying southern Indochina.

	United States freezes Japanese assets.
	Roosevelt recalls Gen. Douglas MacArthur to active service and orders reinforcement of the Philippines.
September	Imperial Conference approves Pearl Harbor attack plan.
October	War minister Hideki Tojo replaces Prince Fumimaro Konoye as prime minister.
December	Japan attacks Pearl Harbor.

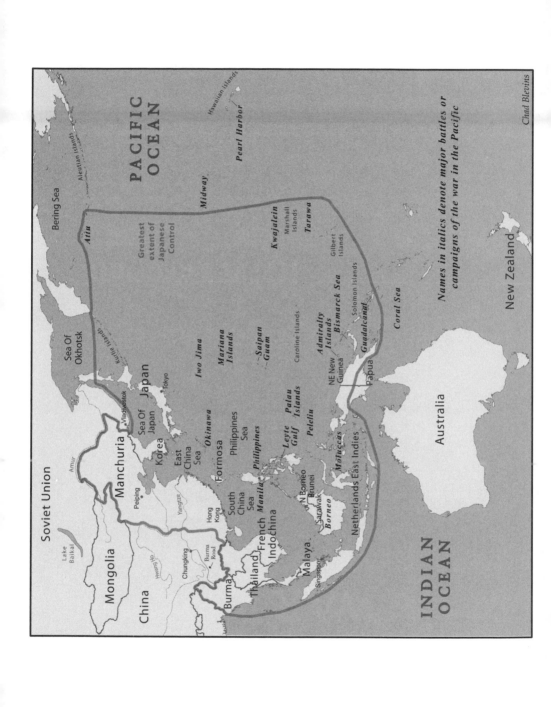

Names in italics denote major battles or
campaigns of the war in the Pacific

Chad Blevins

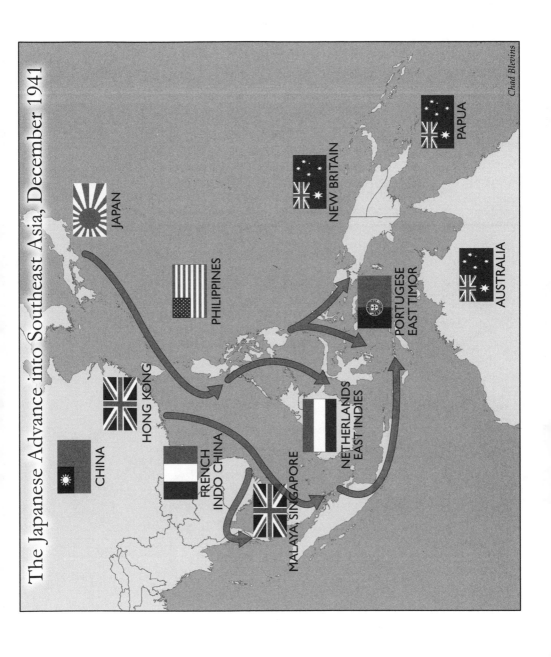

The Japanese Advance into Southeast Asia, December 1941

Chad Blevins

JAPAN

CHINA

HONG KONG

PHILIPPINES

FRENCH
INDO CHINA

MALAYA, SINGAPORE

NETHERLANDS
EAST INDIES

PORTUGESE
EAST TIMOR

NEW BRITAIN

PAPUA

AUSTRALIA

CHAPTER ONE

Introduction

A *"Strategic Imbecility"?*

The Japanese attack on Pearl Harbor continues to perplex. Just weeks after the attack, Prime Minister Winston Churchill declared to a Joint Session of Congress that the attack was "an irrational act" irreconcilable "with prudence or even with sanity."[1] The American naval historian Samuel Eliot Morison called Tokyo's decision for war against the United States "a strategic imbecility."[2] How, in mid-1941, could Japan—militarily mired in China and seriously considering an opportunity for war with the Soviet Union (the Germans had invaded Russia in June)—even think about yet another war, this one against a distant country with a ten-fold industrial superiority? The United States was not only stronger; it lay beyond Japan's military reach. The United States could out-produce Japan in every category of armaments as well as build weapons, such as long-range bombers, that Japan could not; and though Japan could fight a war in East Asia and the Western Pacific, it could not threaten the American homeland. In attacking Pearl Harbor, Japan elected to fight a geographically limited war against an enemy capable, once fully mobilized, of waging a total war against the Japanese home islands themselves. Japan could never be greater than a regional power, whereas the United States had the potential to become—and indeed became—the greatest global power the world had ever seen.

In 1941 the U.S. Chief of Naval Operations, Admiral Harold "Betty" Stark, had a conversation with Admiral Kichisaburo Nomura, the Japanese ambassador to the United States. Stark warned:

If you attack us we will break your empire before we are through with you. While you may have initial success due to timing and surprise, the time will come when you too will have your losses but there will be this great difference. You not only will be unable to make up your losses but will grow weaker as time goes on; while on the other hand we will not only make up our losses but will grow stronger as time goes on. It is inevitable that we shall crush you before we are through with you. [3]

Nomura made no reply.

Did the Japanese recognize the odds against them? What could possibly prompt such a reckless course of action as the attack on Pearl Harbor? Fatalism? Delusional reasoning? Madness? "Was it national *hara-kiri*?"[4] Was there no acceptable alternative to war with the United States in 1941? And if not, how did Tokyo expect to compel the United States to accept Japanese hegemony in East Asia? Did the Japanese have a concept of victory, or at least of avoiding defeat? Or were they simply, as New York congressman Hamilton Fish declared the day after Pearl Harbor, a "stark, raving mad" people who by attacking the United States had "committed military, naval, and national suicide"?[5]

Was the Pacific War inevitable? Could the Japanese have extended their empire into Southeast Asia without attacking the United States? How did the Roosevelt administration, which in late 1941 wanted war with Germany—not Japan—nevertheless stumble into war in the Pacific? What was the connection between Nazi Germany and Imperial Japan, between Nazi aggression in Europe and Japanese aggression in Southeast Asia?

What lessons can be drawn from the Japanese decision for war in 1941? From U.S.-Japanese policy interaction during the months leading to Pearl Harbor? Are there lessons of value to today's national security decision makers?

The Pacific War arose out of Japan's drive for national glory and economic security via the conquest of East Asia and the Roosevelt administration's belief that it could check Japan's bid for an Asian empire via measures short of war. The Japanese sought to free themselves from economic dependence on the United States, whereas the Americans sought to use that dependence to contain Japanese imperial ambitions. The Japanese sought to overturn the territorial status quo in Asia, whereas the United States sought to preserve it. Given the scope of Japan's ambitions, which included the expulsion of Western (and Soviet) power and influence from East Asia, and given Japan's alliance with Nazi Germany (against whom the United States was tacitly allied with Great Britain), war with the United States was probably inevitable by the end of 1941 even though Japanese prospects for winning a war with the United States were minimal.

The disaster that awaited Japan in its war with the United States was rooted in a fatal excess of ambition over power. Japan's imperial aspirations, which included Soviet territory in Northeast Asia as well as China and Western-controlled territory in Southeast Asia, lay beyond Japan's material capacity to seize and sustain. Japan wanted to be a great power of the first rank like the United States, Great Britain, and Germany but lacked the industrial base and military capacity to become one. Moreover, Japan sought both a continental empire over the teeming populations of the Asian mainland as well as a maritime empire in the southwestern Pacific—a tall order given China's sheer size and rising nationalism and the global naval superiority of Great Britain and the United States. Few Japanese leaders fully appreciated the limits of Japan's power; on the contrary, many had wildly exaggerated ideas of Japan's destiny and ability to fulfill it.

The presumption of Japanese irrationality is natural given Japan's acute imperial overstretch in 1941 and the huge disparity between, on the one hand, Japan's industrial base and military power, and on the other hand, America's industrial base and *latent* military power. Dean Acheson, who in 1941 was assistant secretary of state for economic affairs, declared before Pearl Harbor that "no rational Japanese could believe that an attack on us could result in anything but disaster for his country."[6] Secretary of War Henry L. Stimson believed the Japanese, "however wicked their intentions, would have the good sense not to get involved in a war with the United States."[7] Admiral Isoroku Yamamoto certainly had good sense. In October 1940 he warned, "To fight the United States is like fighting the whole world. . . . Doubtless I shall die aboard the *Nagato* [his flagship]. Meanwhile, Tokyo will be burnt to the ground three times."[8] Barely two months before Pearl Harbor, Yamamoto predicted:

> It is obvious that a Japanese-American war will become a protract-
> ed one. As long as the tides of war are in our favor, the United
> States will never stop fighting. As a consequence, the war will con-
> tinue for several years, during which [our] material [resources] will
> be exhausted, vessels and arms will be damaged, and they can be
> replaced only with great difficulties. Ultimately we will not be able
> to contend with [the United States]. As a result of war the people's
> livelihood will become indigent . . . and it is hard not to imagine
> [that] the situation will become out of control. We must not start a
> war with so little chance of success. [9]

Postwar assessments are no less condemnatory. "The Japanese bet, in 1941," wrote French political and social theorist Raymond Aron in 1966, "was *senseless*, since on paper the Empire of the Rising Sun had no chance of winning and could avoid losing only if the Americans were too lazy or cowardly to conquer."[10] Gordon Prange, the late and great historian of Pearl Harbor, called the attack the beginning of "a reckless war it [Japan] could not possibly win."[11] Strategist Edward N. Luttwak contends that the Japanese had no victory options after Pearl Harbor other than "an invasion of California, followed by the conquest of the major centers of American life and culminating with an imposed peace dictated to some collaborating government in Washington." Luttwak ac-knowledges that such a strategy lay fantastically beyond Japan's power, and in fact no Japanese leader ever proposed an invasion of the United States. "So the best Japanese option after Pearl Harbor was to sue im-mediately for peace, bargaining away Japan's ability to resist eventual defeat for some years in exchange for whatever the United States would concede to avoid having to fight for its victory."[12] For strategist Colin Gray, the "Asia-Pacific War of 1941-5 was a conflict that Imperial Japan was *always* going to lose. It remains a cultural and strategic puzzle why so many Japanese military and political leaders endorsed the decision to go to war in 1941 while knowing that fact."[13]

The late Roberta Wohlstetter, in her groundbreaking *Pearl Harbor: Warning and Decision*, denounced the fanciful Japanese thinking behind the decision for war: "Most unreal was their assumption that the United States, with ten times the military potential and a reputation for waging war until unconditional surrender, would after a short struggle accept the annihilation of a considerable part of its naval and air forces and the whole of its power in the Far East."[14] Toshikazu Kase, a Japanese foreign ministry official who was present when General Douglas MacArthur accepted Japan's surrender aboard the battleship USS *Missouri* on September 2, 1945, wondered in retrospect "how it was that Japan, a poor country, had the temerity to wage war against the combination of so many powerful nations. . . . The contest was unequal from the first. [It] was the product of brains fired by sheer madness."[15] Perhaps the most savage indictment is that of Haruo Tohmatsu and H. P. Willmott: "[N]o state or nation has ever been granted immunity from its own stupidity. But Japan's defeat in World War II was awesome. The coalition of powers that it raised against itself, the nature of its defeat across an entire ocean, and the manner in which the war ended represented an astonishing and remarkable, if unintended, achievement on the part of Japan."[16]

Was the Japanese decision for war in 1941 just a matter of stupidity? Can it be dismissed as simply a cultural puzzle? Is it beyond comprehension? Or did it make sense, given the alternatives? And what were those alternatives?

Thucydides famously explained the desire of ancient Athens to retain its empire by declaring that "fear, honor, and interest" were "three of the strongest motives."[17] "Realist" theories of international politics focus on calculations of power and interest as the primary drivers of state behavior, and in so doing tend to discount other factors, such as ideology and pride, that distort "rational" analysis of risks and rewards. Ideology and pride, however, are central to understanding the international behavior of many states, including Japan from 1931 to 1945. For some states, including Imperial Japan and Nazi Germany, ideology and national interest were inseparable. Indeed, the influence of ideology on the foreign policy decision making of the great powers of the twentieth century, especially Imperial Germany, Soviet Russia, Nazi Germany, Imperial Japan, Mao Tse-tung's China, and, yes, the United States, deserves more academic scrutiny than it has received.

It is the central conclusion of this study that *the Japanese decision for war against the United States in 1941 was dictated by Japanese pride and Japan's threatened economic destruction by the United States*. The United States sought to deter Japanese imperial expansion into Southeast Asia by employing its enormous leverage over the Japanese economy; it demanded that Japan withdraw its forces from both Indochina *and* China—in effect that Japan renounce its empire in exchange for a restoration of trade with the United States and acceptance of American principles of international behavior. Observed Sir Basil Henry Liddell Hart in retrospect: "No Government, least of all the Japanese, could be expected to swallow such humiliating conditions, and utter loss of face."[18]

This conclusion excuses neither the attack on Pearl Harbor nor the stupidity of Tokyo's statecraft in the 1930s in placing Japan in a situation where war, surrender, and impoverishment were the only policy choices available. Like Nazi Germany, Japan was, in the decade of the 1930s, a serial aggressor state that eventually brought about its own downfall by picking too many powerful enemies. Japan's attempt to conquer China and to displace Western power in Southeast Asia inevitably provoked armed resistance. Stumbling into a war that Japan was *"always* going to lose" owed much to Japanese racism, fatalism, imperial arrogance, and cultural ignorance. The Japanese confused honor with interest by permitting their imperial ambitions to run hopelessly far ahead of their military capacity to achieve them. Indeed, the Japanese, like the Germans (and later, the Israelis), displayed a remarkable incapacity for sound strategic thinking. They never recognized the limits of their military power, and they were simultaneously mesmerized by short-term operational opportunities and blind to their likely disastrous long-term strategic consequences. How else could Tokyo consider war with the United States *and* the Soviet Union *in addition to* a debilitating, four-year war it did not know how to win in China?

Nor does this study's thesis excuse the savagery of Japanese behavior in East Asia during the 1930s and 1940s or the unwillingness of postwar Japanese governments to acknowledge and atone for that behavior. The Japanese, unlike the Germans, have refused to come to terms with their past wars of conquest and their atrocious treatment of conquered populations, and the argument that the American saturation bombing of Japanese cities culminating in the atomic bombings of Hiroshima and Nagasaki absolves the Japanese of any moral responsibility for their own prior transgressions in East Asia is patently absurd. Many Japanese *were* victims of American violence during World War II, and the mass aerial slaughter of Japanese civilians seems, certainly in retrospect, morally indefensible. But it was not the Americans who sought to conquer all of East Asia, who seized Manchuria, who overran most of China, who invaded Southeast Asia, and who started the Pacific War. Severe U.S. economic sanctioning of Japan in 1941 may have accelerated the slide toward war, but the root cause of the Pacific War was Japan's attempt to conquer East Asia.

In October 2008, Yoshio Tamogami, the chief of staff of the Japanese air force, was relieved of command for writing an essay—"Was Japan an Aggressor Nation?"—in which he justified Japanese colonialism, denied that Japan had waged wars of aggression, and suggested that Roosevelt had lured the Japanese into attacking Pearl Harbor. Tamogami also claimed that many Asia countries "take a positive view of the Greater East Asia War" and that reports of brutality on the part of Japanese soldiers during that war were simply "rumors."[19] The incident was but the latest involving a falsification of the history of Japan's behavior in East Asia in the 1930s and 1940s by a high-ranking Japanese official. Additionally, millions of Japanese, including government officials, continue to pay homage to Japanese war dead at the notorious Yasukuni Shrine each year, even though the shrine venerates fourteen senior military officers convicted of war crimes after Japan formally surrendered.[20] Michael Bess has reminded us that

> Throughout their conquered territories, Japanese soldiers in World War II indulged in an orgy of sadistic violence that leaves the historical observer dumbstruck: in China they routinely raped civilian women, sometimes killing them afterwards; in Singapore they massacred five thousand Chinese by beheading them, shooting

them, or taking them far into the ocean and pushing them overboard to drown; in Hong Kong they bayoneted the doctors, nurses, and patients in hospitals; at Tjepu, in Java, they killed all the captured Dutch men and boys, in many cases chopping off their arms and legs, then gang-raped the women and girls; in the POW camps they freely bayoneted or tortured Australian and British soldiers, a common practice being to tear out their fingernails; in Malaya they tortured English prisoners to death, then cut off their genitals and stuffed them into their mouths, displaying the mutilated corpses on trees; at Manokwari, in New Guinea, they engaged repeatedly in acts of cannibalism, killing Asian POWs and eating their flesh; in Manchuria they performed biological experiments on Chinese men and women, exposing several thousand of them to deadly diseases, and subsequently dissecting many of them while they were still alive. [21]

Like their Nazi allies, the Japanese militarists embraced a virulent race-based Social Darwinism which, though it produced no genocide on the scale of the Holocaust, accounted for the atrocious behavior of Japanese troops throughout Tokyo's Asian empire. The Japanese "saw themselves as the Yamato race, an ancient people of exceptionally pure blood and high culture, destined to lead all other Asians into a glorious future." The central fact about this vision "lay in the fundamental Japanese certainty that the other peoples of Asia were racially inferior . . . and that the Japanese were the only ones who deserved the position of master. The [Greater East Asian Co-Prosperity] 'sphere' was actually a pyramid."[22] Even today, one hears the argument that pressuring Japan to apologize for its past aggression by emulating Germany's remarkable contrition would risk a nationalist backlash in Japan.[23]

All that said, however, it is necessary to observe that the United States was guilty of grievous miscalculation in the Pacific in 1941. It takes at least two parties to transform a political dispute into war. Racism was hardly unique to the Japanese, and Americans were, if anything, even more culturally ignorant of Japan than the Japanese were of the United States. President Roosevelt had a quite negative, stereotyped view of Japan and the Japanese, which was reinforced by a romantic image of the Chinese and his long stint as assistant secretary of the navy (1913–1921), a service that regarded Japan as a dedicated and danger-ous enemy.[24] The conviction—widespread within the Roosevelt admin-istration until the last months of 1941—that no sensible Japanese leader could rationally contemplate war with the United States, blinded key policymakers to the likely consequences of such reckless decisions as the imposition of what amounted to a complete trade embargo of Japan in the summer of 1941. The embargo abruptly deprived Japan of 80 per-cent of its oil requirements, confronting Tokyo with the choice of either submitting to U.S. demands that it give up its empire in China and re-sume its economic dependency on the United States or, alternatively, advancing into resource-rich Southeast Asia and placing its expanded empire on an economically independent foundation. The embargo thus provoked, rather than cowed, Japan. David Kahn has observed that

> American racism and rationalism kept the United States from thinking that Japan would attack it. . . . Japan was not only more distant [than Germany]; since she had no more than half America's population and only one-ninth of America's industrial output, ra-tionality seemed to preclude her attacking the United States. And disbelief in a Japanese attack was reinforced by belief in the supe-riority of the white race. Americans looked upon Japanese as buck-toothed, bespectacled little yellow men, forever photographing things with their omnipresent cameras so they could copy them. Such opinions were held not only by common bigots but by opinion-makers as well. [25]

Indeed, more than a few administration decision makers, Stimson among them, suspected that Germany was behind the Pearl Harbor at-tack. Gordon Prange observed that "It was difficult for these men in Washington to accept the fact that a military operation so swift, so ruth-less, so painfully successful—in a word, so blitzkrieg—in nature did not originate with Hitler."[26]

It was easy to dismiss the Japanese as a serious military challenge. Today, "we can easily forget how little credibility Westerners assigned to the Japanese military in 1941," reminds Jean Edward Smith.

The army had been bogged down in China for four years; Zhukov had made quick work of the garrison in Manchukuo; and the Japanese Navy had not been engaged in battle on the high seas since 1905. "The Japs," as FDR called them, might prevail in Southeast Asia, but they were scarcely seen as a threat to American forces in the Pacific, certainly not to Pearl Harbor, which both the Army and the Navy believed to be impregnable.[27]

Indeed, the crushing defeat of the Imperial Japanese Army (IJA) at Nomohan (Khalkin-Gol) by Soviet armor and artillery in August 1939 revealed the relative technological primitiveness and operational inflexibility of the IJA as well as the comparative weakness of Japan's industrial base.[28] In the years before the war, recounted Prange, "Americans assured one another that Japan was virtually bankrupt, short of raw materials, and hopelessly bogged down in China. It lagged a hundred years behind the times, and in case of a major conflict, its wheel-barrow economy would shatter like a teacup hurled against a brick wall."[29]

The issue of "rationality" is a problematic one. Cultures as disparate as those of the United States and Japan in the 1930s seemingly defy a common standard of rationality. Rationality lies largely in the eyes of the beholder, and "rational" leaders can make horribly mistaken decisions. American examples include the Truman administration's decision to cross the 38th Parallel in Korea in 1950, which witlessly provoked an unnecessary war with China; the Johnson administration's decision to commit U.S. ground combat forces to South Vietnam's defense in 1965; and the George W. Bush administration's baseless decision to invade Iraq in 2003.[30]

Was Churchill's decision to fight on after Dunkirk rational? In May–June 1940 Britain had no means of challenging Hitler's domination of Europe. London had no remaining continental allies (the Soviet Union was Hitler's ally from 1939 to 1941), and the isolationist United States might as well have been on another planet. Britain's only hope of survival, and it was just that—hope—lay in American and Soviet entry into the war, which in turn depended on the chance of profound strategic miscalculations by Germany and Japan. That such miscalculations were forthcoming in Hitler's invasion of the Soviet Union in June 1941 and Japan's attack on the United States in December was, for Churchill, sheer luck. Absent those monumental blunders, Britain would have been finished as a European power and perhaps eventually destroyed by Germany. A "realist" prime minister in May–June 1940 might have explored the possibility of a negotiated departure of Britain from the war by formally accepting German hegemony on the continent in exchange for Hitler's guarantee of the British empire's integrity. Some members of Churchill's cabinet—notably Lord Halifax—are known to have favored exploration of a possible settlement via an approach to Mussolini.[31] At one point even Churchill said he would jump at the chance of forestalling a German invasion of Britain by giving up Malta, Gibraltar, and some African colonies, though he was not prepared to negotiate until the outcome of the coming struggle for air superiority over the British Isles was decided one way or the other. In May–June 1940 the underlying assumption of Churchill and his war cabinet was that eventually there would have to be a negotiated peace with Nazi Germany.[32] (The objective of Germany's unconditional surrender, a fantasy in 1940, had to await Soviet and American entry into the war and the defeat of the Germans at Stalingrad and El Alamein.) Fighting on without allies would have been heroic but futile (one is reminded of Japan's doomed struggle from Okinawa to Nagasaki). Sooner or later, the weight of Germany's military might, reinforced by its conquests in Europe (and continued massive deliveries of grain and other strategically critical raw materials from the Soviet Union), would have proved decisive.

Japan's decision for war was made after months of agonizing internal debate by leaders who recognized America's vast industrial superiority and who, in their more sober moments, suffered few illusions about Japan's chances in a protracted war against America. Japan's leaders did not want war with the United States, but by the fall of 1941 few saw any acceptable alternative. They believed that Japan's invasion of British- and Dutch-controlled Southeast Asia would mean war with the United States and they resigned themselves to it.

Nor did the United States want war with Japan. The Roosevelt administration was committed to stopping Hitler in Europe above all else, and by October 1941 was not only engaged in an undeclared shooting war with Nazi submarines in the North Atlantic but also wedded to a

"Germany-first" strategy in the event of war with all the Axis powers. The last thing Roosevelt wanted was a war in the Pacific. The administration was unwilling to go to war over China and mistakenly believed that it could deter or retard a Japanese advance into Southeast Asia via the retention of powerful naval forces in Hawaii, the imposition of economic sanctions, and the deployment of long-range bombers to the Philippines. It presumed realism and rationality on the part of the Japanese and failed to understand that the sanctions it imposed upon Japan in the summer of 1941 were tantamount to an act of war. "No one during the fall of 1941 wanted war with Japan," observes Jonathan Utley.

> [The] Navy preferred to concentrate on the Atlantic. [The] Army said it needed a few more months before it would be ready in the Philippines. [Secretary of State Cordell] Hull had made the search for peace his primary concern for months. Roosevelt could see nothing to be gained by a war with Japan. Hawks such as Acheson, [Interior secretary Harold] Ickes, and [Treasury secretary Henry] Morgenthau argued that their strong policies would avoid war, not provoke one.[33]

Prange convincingly concluded that "No one who has examined the great mass of historical evidence on Pearl Harbor can doubt that the United States wanted to maintain peace with Japan for as long as possible" because it "wished to remain free to assist Great Britain and defeat Hitler."[34]

The recurring historical revisionism that accuses Roosevelt of having prior knowledge of the attack on Pearl Harbor—indeed, of conspiring to provoke a Japanese attack as a "back door" means of getting the United States into the Second World War—remains unaccompanied by a shred of convincing evidence. The revisionism is an outrageous insult to Roosevelt's patriotism, moral integrity, and love of the American Navy. It also runs afoul of simple logic—e.g., if Roosevelt knew about Pearl Harbor in advance, why did he not order the U.S. Pacific Fleet out to sea? He still would have gotten the war he "wanted" without so many warships sunk or damaged.

What follows is a detailed examination of the foreign policy interaction between Japan and the United States that led to Japan's decision for war in the fall of 1941. The focus is on the critical months separating the fall of France in late June 1940 and Japan's momentous decision, taken in early July 1941, to expand her empire into the "South Seas" (Southeast Asia) even at the risk of war with the United States and Great Britain. The following chapter, "Sources of Japanese-American Tension," identifies and discusses historical sources of antagonism between the two countries that fueled the slide toward war in 1941. Roots as well as expressions of hostility included: American racism and immigration policies, the Open Door Policy and American moralism, naval competition, Japan's seizure of Manchuria and U.S. refusal to recognize its conversion into the puppet state of Manchukuo, Japanese aggression in China, Japan's alliance with Nazi Germany, Japan's manifest imperial ambitions in Southeast Asia, and U.S. economic sanctioning of Japan.

Chapter 3, "Japanese Aggression and U.S. Policy Responses, 1937–1941," examines Japan's aggression in China and Indochina and U.S. responses to it, culminating in the Roosevelt administration's imposition of total shutoff of U.S. exports to Japan. Roosevelt rightly believed that Japan's occupation of southern Indochina in July 1941 presaged an advance against the oil-rich Dutch East Indies and even British Malaya and Singapore and sought to deter it by employing America's enormous economic leverage over Japan. The administration subsequently demanded that Japan evacuate both Indochina and China as the price for ending the sanctions. But Japan refused and began planning for war.

Chapter 4, "Japanese Assumptions and Decision Making," explores how the Japanese approached war with the United States. They made a number of assumptions, some realistic, others not: that the war in Europe would continue to tie down British and Soviet military power; that Great Britain and the United States were strategically indivisible; that time was working against Japan; that Japan had little chance of winning a long war with the United States; that Japan could raise the blood and treasure costs of a war with the United States to the point of convincing the Americans to settle for less than complete victory; and that superior Japan martial prowess could offset America's material advantage. All but one of these assumptions encouraged a decision for war, which was finally taken by a Japanese government leadership dominated by senior military officers and thoroughly militarized civilians.

Chapter 5, "Failed Deterrence," assesses the reasons why neither the Japanese nor the Americans succeeded in deterring one another from going to war. The Japanese hoped their September 1940 military alliance with Nazi Germany would deter the United States from forc ibly interfering with the extension of their empire into Southeast Asia, whereas the Roosevelt administration hoped that economic sanctioning accompanied by a U.S. military buildup in the Philippines would deter Japan from moving south. The United States was not deterred by Japanese threats because Americans were confident they could win any war with Japan, and the Japanese were not deterred by U.S. threats because they preferred death before dishonor.

Chapter 6, "Was the Pacific War Inevitable?" reviews the Japanese and American miscalculations that led to war. At the root of Japan's race toward disaster was a refusal to recognize the fatal disparity between Japan's imperial ambitions, which encompassed not only China and Southeast Asia but also the Soviet Far East, and her industrial and military capacity to fulfill those ambitions. On the American side, perhaps the most consequential miscalculation was the belief on the part of key foreign policymakers that the Japanese would not risk war because, surely, they recognized they could never win a war with the United States.

The final chapter, "The Enduring Lessons of 1941," extracts lessons from the Japanese-American interaction of that critical year that continue to harbor particular relevance for today's national security decision makers. Those lessons are: that fear and honor, "rational" or not, can motivate as much as interest; that there is no substitute for knowledge of a potential adversary's history and culture; that deterrence lies in the mind of the deterree, not the deterrer; that strategy must always inform and guide operations; that economic sanctioning is an inherently hostile act and can be tantamount to an act of war; that the presumption of moral or spiritual superiority can fatally discount the consequences of an enemy's material superiority; and the "inevitable" war easily becomes a self-fulfilling prophecy.

CHAPTER TWO

Sources of Japanese-American Tension

U.S.-Japanese relations foundered during the 1930s on numerous shoals as Japan moved toward dictatorship and war after a decade of flirtation with democracy and internationalism. Long-standing contentious issues included: American racism and immigration policies, the Open Door policy and American moralism, and naval competition. Others of newer vintage were: U.S. nonrecognition of the Japanese puppet state of Manchukuo (Manchuria), Japanese aggression in China, Japan's military alliance with Hitler, Japan's imperial ambitions in Southeast Asia, and U.S. embargoes on Japanese trade.

The foundation of the Pacific War of 1941–1945 was a fundamental dispute over both ends and means. Whereas the United States was committed to preserving the territorial status quo in the Far East and to the principle of peaceful change, Japan sought to overturn the status quo and was prepared to do so by force. The Japanese wanted to dominate East Asia. To do so, however, meant not only subjugating China but also expelling Western power and influence from the region, and it was hardly likely that the Chinese or the Western powers would give way without a fight. The Japanese view was expressed in a document that special envoy Saburo Kurusu handed to Secretary of State Cordell Hull on December 7, 1941, before Hull learned of the attack on Pearl Harbor:

> It is impossible not to reach the conclusion that the American Government desires to maintain and strengthen, in coalition with Great

Britain and other Powers [the] dominant position it has hitherto occupied not only in China but in other areas of East Asia. It is a fact of history that the countries of East Asia for the past hundred years or more have been compelled to accept the *status quo* under the Anglo-American policy of imperialistic exploitation and to sacrifice themselves to the prosperity of the two nations. The Japanese Government cannot tolerate the perpetuation of such a situation since it directly runs counter to Japan's fundamental policy to enable all nations to enjoy each its proper place in the world.[1]

Four months earlier, Kaname Wakasugi, charge d'affairs at the Japanese embassy in Washington, explained to Acting Secretary of State Sumner Welles why Japan had to establish an empire in East Asia:

He said that when Japan first awoke in the middle of the last century from her long sleep of isolation, she found herself completely surrounded by the imperialistic encroachments which occidental nations had made, not only in China, but in all the Pacific region as well. He said that the United States had been a rapidly expanding and growing country but that Japan was likewise a rapidly expanding country, obviously not on the same scale as the United States, but nonetheless on the same general trend. He said that the Japanese people could not indefinitely be confined to their own poor land and that they had to find, in view of their ever increasing birth rate and their rapidly rising power as a great nation in the world, some means of expanding outside their own territories. At the very moment the Japanese people were beginning to realize their situation along these lines, he said, the other great powers of the world had been undertaking exactly the same kind of action, by acquiring colonies and dominating other less advanced peoples, which we, the United States, were now reproaching the Japanese people for undertaking.[2]

Harry Wray points out that "On the way to imperialism Japan learned its lessons well. Japanese leaders presumed that imperialism was the equivalent of being modern and civilized. . . . Japan saw itself as a 'respectable imperialist,' and was disappointed by signs that its expansionist behavior was not universally accepted by the Great Powers."[3] In Hull's view, expressed in congressional testimony in early 1941:

It has been clear throughout that Japan has been actuated from the start by broad and ambitious plans for establishing herself in a dominant position in the entire region of the Eastern Pacific. Her leaders have openly declared their determination to achieve and maintain that position by force of arms and thus to make themselves master of an area containing almost one-half of the entire population of the world. As a consequence, they would have arbitrary control of the sea and trade routes of that region.[4]

As early as 1934, Joseph C. Grew, U.S. ambassador to Japan, presciently warned the State Department that

Their [the Japanese] aim is to obtain trade control and eventually predominant political influence in China, the Philippines, the Straits Settlement [Malaya], Siam [Thailand] and the Dutch East Indies . . . one step at a time, as in Korea and Manchuria, pausing intermittently to consolidate and then continuing as soon as the intervening obstacles can be overcome by diplomacy and force. With such dreams of empire cherished by many, and with an army and navy capable of taking the bit in their own teeth and running away with it regardless of the restraining influence of the saner heads of Government in Tokyo . . . we would be reprehensively somnolent if we were to trust the security of treaty restraints or international comity to safeguard our own interests.

Grew added:

When Japanese speak of Japan's being the "stabilizing factor" and the "guardian of peace" of Asia, what they have in mind is a Pax Japonica with eventual complete commercial control and, in the

minds of some, eventual complete political control of East Asia.
. . . There is a swashbuckling temper in the country . . . which can
lead Japan during the next few years . . . to any extremes unless the
saner minds in the Government prove able to cope with it and to
restrain the country from national suicide.[5]

U.S. Racism and Immigration Policies. The late George F. Kennan once
observed that the "long and unhappy story" of deteriorating Japanese-
American relations during the 1920s and 1930s was exacerbated because
"we would repeatedly irritate and offend the sensitive Japanese by our
immigration policies and the treatment of people of Japanese lineage,
and of oriental lineage in general, in specific localities in this country."[6]
California was a major offender. In 1906 the San Francisco Board of
Education voted to segregate Japanese and other Orientals from non-
Oriental students. Though President Theodore Roosevelt persuaded the
board to rescind its decision, he also extracted from Japan a pledge to
restrict further Japanese emigration to the United States. In 1913 California banned Japanese from owning land in the state.

In 1919 the Japanese delegation to the Versailles Conference request-
ed that a declaration of racial equality be inserted into the preamble of
the League of Nations Covenant. As the only non-white major power
at the conference, Japan foresaw the possibility of being treated as less
than equal in an organization dominated by Europeans and Americans.
The language the Japanese proposed was simple: "The equality of nations being a basic principle of the League of Nations, the High Contracting Parties agree to accord, as soon as possible, to all alien nationals
of States members of the League, equal and just treatment in every respect, making no distinction, either in law or in fact, on account of their
race or nationality."[7] The British and U.S. delegations, led by President
Woodrow Wilson, a profound racist with respect to African Americans
in his own country, refused to accept the declaration. Though a majority
of the delegates present voted in favor of the racial equality clause, Wilson overturned the vote by declaring, nonsensically, that opposition to
the measure was too strong to permit anything other than a unanimous
vote for passage. Worse still, when the Japanese responded by threaten-

ing not to sign the Versailles Treaty, Wilson sought to conciliate them by endorsing Japan's claim to defeated Germany's former territorial and commercial concessions on China's Shantung Peninsula, which Japan had seized during the war. This attempt to appease the Japanese by giving them former German concessions that rightfully should have been returned to China outraged Chinese and American opinion alike (China refused to sign the Versailles Treaty) and demonstrated an unsavory American willingness to sacrifice what remained of China's territorial integrity in order to appease Japan. The incorporation of the concessions transfer to Japan in Article 156 of the treaty contributed greatly to the U.S. Senate's defeat of the treaty in 1920.[8]

In 1922 the U.S. Supreme Court ruled that no Oriental immigrant could become a naturalized American citizen, and two years later the U.S. Congress passed, as part of an immigration bill, an Exclusion Act that banned all Japanese immigration. The law remained on the books until 1965. (Discrimination against Japanese continued after the Japanese attack on Pearl Harbor when, in February 1942, President Franklin D. Roosevelt signed the infamous Executive Order 9066, which effectively stripped 110,000 Japanese nationals and American *citizens* of Japanese ancestry of their property and mandated their internment in what amounted to prison camps.)

This record of anti-Japanese racism, much of it embedded in notions of white racial superiority and fears of a "Yellow Peril" (i.e., the belief, especially strong in California and the other the American West Coast states, that mass immigration from Asia threatened white wages and living standards[9]), certainly never excused Japanese racism, which was just as profound with respect to the Koreans, Chinese, and other victims of Japanese aggression in Asia. But it did serve as a toxic undercurrent in a relationship that was always going to be hard to manage once Japan abandoned internationalism in favor of militarism. Kenneth Pyle has written that discrimination against Japanese immigrants in the United States "became an open sore on the Japanese psyche," and that "Japan's self-image as one of the world's five great powers was constantly undermined by the treatment of Japanese immigrants as second-class citizens in the Anglo-Saxon countries."[10] But American racism also had more direct strategic consequences: it encouraged an underestimation of Japan's capacity to wage modern war and the technical skills of its armed forces (particularly its navy and fighter pilots), which in turn encouraged an underestimation of Japan's willingness to defy Roosevelt administration attempts at coercive diplomacy during the crisis years of 1939–1941.

Indeed, it is difficult, especially looking back from the early twenty-first century and from an America that elected its first African American president, to comprehend the influence of racial prejudice on elite and public opinion during World War II and the years leading up to its outbreak. "World War II was not a race war, but it was—to an extent that is often overlooked—a conflict in which race played a central role from start to finish and in every theater of combat," observes Michael Bess. "Racial ideas shaped both German and Japanese war aims, and helped spur these two peoples to take the aggressive actions that precipitated military hostilities." On the Allied side, racial prejudices "led to a gross underestimation of Japanese capabilities in 1941—a misperception for which Britain and the United States paid dearly in December 1941 and the early months of 1942."[11]

The Open Door Policy and American Moralism. By the end of the nineteenth century, China—weakened by war, revolution, and the steady encroachment of avaricious European and Japanese imperialism—stood on the verge of being partitioned into colonies or otherwise exclusive commercial zones that would have denied the United States continued access to the lucrative China trade. Afraid of being shut out, the McKinley administration's secretary of state, John Hay, in what became known as the first Open Door Note, issued a circular letter in September 1899 to the great powers involved in China in which he urged them not to discriminate, within their own spheres of influence, against the trade of other states. The following year, in the wake of U.S. participation in an international expeditionary force that suppressed the Boxer Rebellion that had laid siege to the foreign legations in Beijing, Hay issued a second Open Door Note in which he declared it to be the policy of the United States to promote "permanent safety and peace in China, preserve Chinese territorial and administrative entity . . . and safeguard for the world the principle of equal and impartial trade with all parts of the Chinese empire."[12] The Open Door Policy was enshrined as international law in the Nine-Power Treaty of 1922, in which the major imperial powers in China pledged equality of rights and access to the treaty ports within their respective spheres of influence. The treaty lacked any enforcement mechanisms, however, and the Japanese subsequently and repeatedly violated the treaty with impunity.

U.S. concern for China's territorial integrity was rooted in the desire for continued trade access. Neither Hay nor any of his successors prior to World War II challenged the unequal treaties the other powers had imposed upon China at the point of a gun. Nor was the United States prepared to use or even threaten force to uphold China's integrity or preserve U.S. commercial access to China. The myth nonetheless arose, at least in the United States, that America, "in a single act of beneficence at a critical point in China's history saved it from further plunder by the European powers and Japan."[13] Americans came to see themselves as China's natural friends and U.S. behavior in China as morally superior to any other outside power. Kennan observed that "the American public found no difficulty in accepting [the Open Door Notes] as a major diplomatic achievement," and it became "the established opinion of the American public that here, in this episode of the Open Door Notes, a tremendous blow had been struck for the triumph of American principles in international society—an American blow for an American idea."[14]

Kennan correctly identified the Open Door Notes as a reflection of an American "tendency to achieve [its] foreign policy objectives by inducing other governments to sign up to professions of high moral and legal principle."[15] With respect to Japan the tendency persisted right up until the attack on Pearl Harbor. The United States remained committed, at least in loudly professed principle, to China's territorial and administrative integrity, and as Japan moved toward militarism and an expanded empire in China in the 1930s the United States continued to insist that Japan adhere to the principles of a liberal international order. The belief that America was morally exceptional among states was (and remains) a powerful influence on U.S. foreign policy—witness President George W. Bush's embrace of the neoconservative discourse on America's role in the world in the wake of the terrorist attacks on the United States on September 11, 2001. Yet to the extent that it has manifested itself in sermons to predatory states about the sanctity of international law and proper principles of international behavior, it is more or less irrelevant in dealing with the challenges of aggression. Foreign policy moralism also blinds its proponents to specific local circumstances and practical considerations. This was especially true of Secretary of State Cordell Hull in his dealings with Japan. "Hull viewed the world in terms of moral principles," observes Robert Divine. "To Hull diplomacy was the art of preaching, not of negotiation."[16] Consider Hull's portrayal, in postwar testimony, of U.S.-Japanese relations in 1941:

> The whole issue presented was whether Japan would yield in her avowed movement of conquest or whether we would yield the fundamental principles for which we stood in the Pacific and all over the world. By midsummer of 1941 we were pretty well satisfied that the Japanese were determined to continue with their course of expansion by force. We had made it clear to them that we were standing by our principles. It was evident, however, that they were playing for the chance that we might be overawed into yielding by their threats of force. They were armed to the teeth and we knew they would attack whenever and wherever they pleased. If by chance we should have yielded our fundamental principles, Japan probably would not have attacked for the time being—at least not until she had consolidated the gains she would have made without fighting. There was never any question of this country forcing the Japanese to fight. The question was whether this country was ready to sacrifice its principles. [17]

In April 1941, as Japanese aggression in China continued and the war clouds darkened over the Pacific, Hull began to insist on Japanese adherence to four principles as the basis for negotiation of U.S.-Japanese differences: respect for the territorial integrity of all nations, non-interference in the affairs of other countries, support for the principle of equality—including equality of commercial opportunity—and non-disturbance of the status quo in the Pacific except by peaceful means.[18] Because Japan had been a serial violator of all these principles since it began carving out an empire on the Asian mainland in the 1890s, Hull was essentially asking the Japanese to commit imperial suicide. Hull's principles offered no solution to such problems as China's weakness and Japan's expanding population and lack of natural resources. Nor did they acknowledge that Japan's interests on the Asian mainland and in the Western Pacific were far more important to the Japanese than U.S. interests there were to the Americans. Small wonder that the Japanese found Hull's principles tantamount to a demand for surrender as well as flagrantly hypocritical, since all Japan was trying to do was to create for itself the kind of colonial empire the British, French, Dutch, and the Portuguese already possessed. "Everywhere Japan turned it was greeted by talks of quarantine, moral embargo, sanctity of international law, open door, and the like," observes David J. Lu. "Japan's answer to these public pronouncements by Washington was the Monroe Doctrine for East Asia, which implied that the United States should recognize Japan's domination over China."[19]

The Japanese were neither the first nor the last people for whom America's foreign policy moralism was both mystifying and galling. Kenneth Pyle has pointed out that the Japanese were hard-headed realists seeking to maximize Japan's power and status and "had no legacy of transcendental and universal values through which to understand international liberalism. The very idea that a nation must be governed by abstract principles was scarcely credible." As for Hull and the international situation in 1940–1941, "[t]o the Japanese leaders, the assertion of self-determination, territorial integrity, and the Open Door as principles of universal validity flew in the face of reality when applied to a weak and chaotic Asia."[20] Lecturing the Japanese on their behavior in Asia was about as effective as lecturing Hitler on his behavior in Europe.

Naval Competition. Naval competition was both an expression of U.S.-Japanese tensions and a direct contributor to the Japanese decision for war with the United States. Though the competition was regulated during the 1920s by an arms control regime, it degenerated during the following decade into an unrestrained—and for Japan, ultimately fatal— arms race as Tokyo cast off internationalism and withdrew from naval arms control. By late 1941 the Imperial Japanese Navy (IJN) dominated the Western Pacific, including the waters surrounding the Philippine Islands, a U.S. territorial possession scheduled for political independence in 1946. In contrast, U.S. naval power was tightly stretched between the Atlantic and Pacific oceans, with the U.S. Pacific Fleet stationed in the Central Pacific at Hawaii.

Japan emerged as a major naval power in the Pacific in the wake of its victory over China in the Sino-Japanese War of 1894–1895. Japanese naval power attracted a defensive alliance with Great Britain in 1902 (directed against Russian expansionism in the Far East), which was followed by the Russo-Japanese War of 1904–1905 culminating in Japan's stunning victory over Russia's Baltic Fleet in the Tsushima Strait. The IJN continued to grow through World War I and after. By 1920 it ranked a distant third, behind the British and American navies. In 1921, to avoid a costly international naval race, the United States invited Britain, Japan, France, and Italy to a conference in Washington, where U.S. Secretary of State Charles Evans Hughes proposed limits on total battleship tonnage for each country. After considerable negotiation the conferees agreed to the Washington Naval Treaty (also known as the Five-Power Treaty) of 1922, which limited the total capital ship (battleship) tonnage of each of the signatories to the following: 500,000 tons each for Great Britain and the United States; 300,000 tons for Japan; and 175,000 tons each from France and Italy. The resulting ratio for the top three naval powers was thus 10:10:6. The treaty established similar ratios for total aircraft carrier tonnage (aircraft carriers were not regarded as capital ships at the time). The treaty also prohibited construction of warships over 35,000 tons and naval guns in excess of 16 inches in diameter. Thus Japan accepted a 6:10 inferiority to the United States in battleship tonnage, an inferiority that was offset by the fact that the U.S. Navy had obligations in both the Atlantic and Pacific, whereas the IJN was a one-ocean force. The inferiority was also somewhat offset by treaty provisions banning construction of new fortifications or naval bases in most of the Pacific, including the Philippines.

The treaty effectively guaranteed Japanese naval domination of East Asian waters, including those surrounding the weakly defended Philippines. "The Japanese were left with a clear local superiority in the Far East" and "in a position of total domination of the coast and approaches to China."[21] The United States was two decades away from having a genuine two-ocean navy (i.e., the capacity to simultaneously defeat major naval challenges in the Atlantic and Pacific) and lacked the bases and fortifications in the Philippines to support and protect a large naval presence in East Asian waters (U.S. naval forces deployed to the Pacific operated from the American West Coast). The treaty also benefited Japan in another very important way: it limited U.S. naval tonnage to a fraction of American shipbuilding potential. Yamamoto embraced the treaty ratio for precisely that reason, declaring that the 10:10:6 "ratio works just fine for us; it is a treaty to restrict the *other* parties."[22] He clearly understood that Japan would be swamped in an all-out naval race with the United States, whereas the treaty's 10:10:6 ratio and ban of new fortifications ensured Japanese naval domination of East Asia. (Even before 1922, however, IJN hardliners had determined that Japan required at least a 70 percent ratio of naval tonnage to that of the United States, and the 70 percent ratio became dogma for the next thirty years.[23])

Moreover, Japanese naval strategy could accommodate a significant inferiority in overall capitol ship tonnage vis-à-vis the United States. In the event of war with America, the Japanese planned to lure U.S. naval forces across the Pacific into an ambush in East Asian waters—just as the IJN had ambushed Russia's Baltic Fleet off the Korean coast in 1905. The Japanese believed that California-based U.S. naval forces would form up and sail across the Pacific into East Asian waters to protect the Philippines. A Japanese attack on the Philippines would almost certainly provoke such deployment; it would not only deny the use of Manila Bay to the U.S. Navy but also "help induce the American fleet to come to an early decisive battle in the Western Pacific."[24] Given the inherent logistical toll of traversing the great distances separating the American West Coast and the Southwestern Pacific as well as the opportunities to further whittle down U.S. naval forces via submarine and air attacks as they moved through the Japanese-controlled Mariana, Marshall, and Caroline island groups, the IJN might actually enjoy a quantitative superiority at the time and place of the climactic battle.[25] Japanese fleet exercises throughout the 1920s and most of the 1930s were predicated on this strategy. The plan was simple. The Japanese "would use land-based aircraft from neighboring bases and island groups, plus the fleet, to support formations and bases brought under attack," describes Pacific War historian H. P. Willmott, "the point being that the various parts of the defense—the forward base, the supporting elements, and the fleet component—would be mutually supportive and would together provide overall numerical superiority relative to a [U.S.] amphibious assault certain to possess initial numerical superiority over any single part of the Japanese defense."[26] Both U.S. and Japanese naval leaders believed that the United States required at least a 2:1 ratio in overall fleet tonnage to prevail over the IJN in the Western Pacific.[27]

Not all IJN leaders, however, favored the Washington Treaty limits. Some, like Yamamoto, understood that the treaty put a greater brake on America's potential naval shipbuilding than on Japan's, but believed that Japan should be permitted a ratio to the United States higher than 6:10. Others regarded anything less than equality of tonnage with Great Britain and the United States as an unacceptable affront to national honor and Japan's aspirations for great power status. Discontent became apparent at the London Naval Conference of 1930, which was convened to consider limitations on cruisers and other warships not covered by the Washington Treaty. Japan insisted on a 7:10 tonnage ratio for cruisers and destroyers until 1936 (when the 1930 treaty limits would be considered for renewal) and parity in submarine tonnage. Though the United States initially opposed the new ratio, it eventually acquiesced. Unfortunately for the future of naval arms control, the 7:10 ratio was strongly opposed within the IJN by radicals who rejected any limitations on Japanese warship construction. As Japan became increasingly isolated internationally after its seizure of Manchuria and subsequent withdrawal from the League of Nations, the IJN divided into a "treaty faction" favoring continued adherence to negotiate limits and a "fleet faction" that demanded a minimum 7:10 ratio in capital ships, an 8:10 ratio in heavy cruisers, and parity in light cruisers, destroyers, and submarines.[28] By mid-1934 the fleet faction had pushed the treaty faction aside and was demanding parity in all categories of naval construction.

It was determined to break out of the London limits and was perfectly prepared to withdraw from the naval arms control process altogether.

Japan's announcement in late 1934 that it would not attend the London Naval Conference of 1936 effectively signaled her refusal to accept any limitations, quantitative or qualitative, on future naval building. In contrast to the United States, which actually ceased new warship construction during the worst years of the Great Depression, Japan had already built up to existing treaty limits. But by 1940, Japan, having decided in 1936 to mobilize its population and economy for total war, increased naval construction by a whopping 500 percent—or 420,000 tons.[29] Moreover, Japan effectively shielded most of its new construction from public view as well as from the prying eyes of Western intelligence agencies. The result was a Japanese navy in 1941 that surprised its Western competitors by its technical modernity and firepower (the battleships *Yamato* and *Musashi*, each displacing 62,300 tons and mounting nine 18-inch guns, were the largest in the world) and that enjoyed numerical parity or superiority in the Pacific over the combined naval forces of the United States, Great Britain, the Netherlands, and Free France. Though, in the Pacific, Japan deployed one less battleship and six fewer submarines than her combined Western enemies, she had parity in cruisers and an advantage of thirteen more destroyers. In the critical category of aircraft carriers Japan had an overpowering 10:3 superiority.[30]

Japan's boycott of the London Conference and attempted naval breakout predictably excited American suspicions and spurred U.S. naval rearmament, which began in earnest in 1938 and accelerated dramatically in 1940. By the time of the attack on Pearl Harbor, the United States had launched a naval construction program that dwarfed Japan's, and in so doing provided Japan a powerful incentive for preventive war before the naval balance shifted hopelessly against Tokyo.

At the root of Japan's naval breakout was revulsion over being treated as an inferior by Great Britain and the United States. In 1935, Admiral Kichisaburo Nomura, an acquaintance of Franklin Roosevelt who became ambassador to the United States in 1941, published an article in *Foreign Affairs* entitled "Japan's Demand for Naval Equality" in which he declared that the Washington Treaty's 10:10:6 ratio in capital ships "was a decided blow to the self-respect of the Japanese people."[31] Japan, he said, had become convinced that "so long as she suffers from the stigma of the [ratio] she cannot fulfill her mission of preserving order and peace in the Far East. This ratio must be abolished, and Japan granted a position of equality with other Powers."[32] Nomura went on to note that the United States enjoyed complete and unchallenged military hegemony in the Western Hemisphere via "the Monroe Doctrine—a measure calculated to forestall any new European intervention in the affairs of the American continents," and that "[s]uch being the case, it is hardly conceivable that the United States would attempt to contest the balance of power with Japan in the latter's own 'backyard.'"[33] Nomura concluded, in a clear reference to Great Britain and the United States:

> What we would ask of the highly armed Powers is that they cast aside the dictatorial attitude of forcing an inferior ratio upon our country, and that they be magnanimous enough to discuss with us the problems at hand in a spirit of fair play and on a basis of equality in all things. Just as the basis of equality and the principle of equal opportunity govern the relations between individuals today, so must they govern the relations between countries.[34]

The disparity between the Japanese and American security environments remained a constant in Japanese diplomatic argumentation. In July 1941 Nomura declared to a State Department audience that the United States "was in the safest condition as far as national defense was concerned, for there was no fear at all . . . of being attacked by other countries." He pointed out that the United States was "on especially friendly terms with Canada," and claimed that "Mexico was just like what Manchukuo was to Japan, that the countries south of Panama, not to speak of north of it, were gradually coming within the sphere of American influence." There was simply "no comparison between the United States and Japan in point of national security."[35]

U.S. Nonrecognition of Manchuria. In September 1931 Japanese army forces in Manchuria blew up some track on a Japanese-owned railroad and proclaimed that it had been an attack by Chinese military forces.

They used what became known as the Manchurian Incident as a pretext for seizing much of Manchuria, a territory traditionally part of China but for the preceding several decades disputed by Russia and Japan as well. Tokyo subsequently converted Manchuria into a puppet state, Manchukuo, under the nominal rule of the last emperor of China's Qing dynasty, Pu Yi, who occupied the newly created throne as the "emperor" of Manchuria. The United States responded by refusing to extend diplomatic recognition to Manchukuo. Henry Stimson, who in 1931 was President Hoover's secretary of state, wanted to impose economic sanctions on the Japanese for their aggression in Manchuria, but Hoover would not support sanctions. Instead, taking up an idea first proposed by Hoover, Stimson in January 1932 proclaimed what became known as the Stimson Doctrine of Nonrecognition. The doctrine denied U.S. diplomatic recognition of territorial changes obtained by the use of force and that violated the Open Door policy.[36] The Stimson Doctrine had no influence on the Japanese, who proceeded to conquer all of Manchuria. Nor did a League of Nations report which criticized Japan for using excessive force in Manchuria and also supported nonrecognition of Manchukuo. Japan's response was to withdraw from the League.

The U.S.-led condemnation of Japan's takeover of Manchuria alienated Japan and constituted a major factor in Japan's decision to abandon the policy of internationalism it had reluctantly embraced after World War II. Only four years separated Japan's withdrawal from the League and its boycott of the London Naval Conference of 1936. Indeed, it is possible that the Japanese interpreted the Stimson Doctrine as a sign of weakness—another example of moralist barking with no bite. Japan was highly dependent on the United States for critical commodities and industrial items; yet the United States, which had minimal interests in Manchuria, did not invoke its powerful economic leverage, choosing instead to merely preach. Historian Andrew J. Crozier believes that "from this time [the proclamation of the Stimson Doctrine] onwards Japan and the USA were locked into postures that in due course would lead to war, for Japan would not back down and neither would the USA accept the changes in the Far East that Japan had imposed and wished to impose by force."[37]

Japanese Aggression in China and U.S. Assistance to Chiang Kai-shek's Nationalist Government. No issue excited more American hostility toward Japan than Japan's aggression in China. Many Americans had a romantic view of China fanned by such popular novels as Pulitzer and Nobel Prize–winner Pearl S. Buck's *The Good Earth* (1931), *Sons* (1932), *A House Divided* (1935), and *China Sky* (1941). The approximately 2,500 American missionaries in China during the 1930s contributed heavily to "the stimulation of public opinion extremely sympathetic to the Chinese and highly favorable to an American policy of partisanship for China."[38] As Henry Stimson noted in his 1936 book, *The Far Eastern Crisis — Recollections and Observations:*

> Throughout [the] years, in almost every fair-sized American community, particularly throughout our North Eastern and mid-Western states, there had been situated one or more churches, each of which was in whole or in part supporting one or more foreign missionaries, a large percentage of whom were working in China. The news of the work of these missionaries, coming through their reports and letters reached a large number of people living in almost every quarter of the land.[39]

Many of the missionaries were resident in coastal or adjacent provinces of China, most of which were, by late 1941, occupied by Japanese forces. Driven out of China, returning missionaries were predictably hostile to Japan and carried home stories that enraged American audiences. "Of all the stories told by missionaries in China," observed John Masland on the eve of Pearl Harbor, "none has been reiterated with so much emotional appeal as those which describe conditions brought about by the Japanese invasion. . . . Missionaries have served to keep China's suffering before the American public." Masland also pointed out that in contrast to their portrayal of Japanese aims and behavior, missionaries promoted "highly favorable accounts of the Chinese Government and high Chinese officials," including the fact that many officials had been educated in Christian institutions "and that many of them are themselves Christians, including Generalissimo Chiang Kai-shek and his wife."[40] China missionaries became a powerful informal lobby favoring military assistance to China and opposing continued U.S. exports to Japan.

Roosevelt was also sympathetic to China and, certainly after the Japanese invasion of China, hostile to Japan. His maternal grandfather, Warren Delano, had amassed a fortune in the China trade, and his mother had lived in Hong Kong as a child. At Harvard he made the acquaintance of Japanese students, one of whom, Roosevelt later recalled, told him of a hundred-year Japanese expansion plan that included Korea, Manchuria, China, and eventually Australia, New Zealand, and Hawaii. As assistant secretary of the navy during Woodrow Wilson's presidency, Roosevelt served an institution that regarded the Japanese navy as a threat and planned for war with Japan. And as president-elect, and over the objections of two of his key advisers (Raymond Moley and Rexford Tugwell), he met with outgoing Secretary of State Stimson and agreed to embrace Stimson's nonrecognition of Manchukuo.[41]

Americans saw China as a helpless victim of rapacious Western and Japanese imperialism and themselves as champions of China's territorial integrity. The expanded Japanese war in China that began in 1937, accompanied as it was by widely published photographs of Japanese bombing of Chinese cities in American newspapers and magazines such as *Life*, aroused public opinion against Japan more than any other issue. Cordell Hull repeatedly protested to the Japanese ambassador about "the unprovoked bombing and machine-gunning of civilian populations," at one point handing the ambassador a detailed list of Japanese air attacks on civilians as well as American property.[42] From 1937 until the summer of 1941, American public sentiment for the harsh economic sanctioning of Japan for its depredations in China ran significantly ahead of what the Roosevelt administration was prepared to endorse. Though the administration was sympathetic to China's plight, it was increasingly preoccupied with events in Europe and did not wish to provoke an expansion of Japanese aggression.

Japanese aggression in China was inherently hostile to declared U.S. interests because it threatened China's territorial integrity and American commercial access to China. It also portended the establishment in China, as in Manchuria, of a vast, closed empire that would make a mockery of even a pretense of China's independence. The Roosevelt administration did not believe that U.S. interests in China were worth a war with Japan, but it did come to believe that Japan's war in China, though morally reprehensible, was a strategic boon insofar as it tied down Japanese military resources that might otherwise be employed northward against the Soviet Union or southward against British Malaya, Singapore, the Dutch East Indies, and the Philippines. This made China a tacit U.S. ally against Japan. However, though the United States recognized the Nationalist Government of Chiang Kai-shek, it was not in a position to provide it much financial or military assistance. Until the outbreak of the Pacific War, U.S. war production was stretched thinly between servicing the needs of American rearmament and the provision of Lend-Lease military assistance to Great Britain and the Soviet Union.[43] Nevertheless, by the fall of 1941 the United States had approved modest loans to China, sent a military mission to the Nationalist Government capital in Chungking, and declared China eligible for Lend-Lease assistance. It was also permitting American pilots to join the newly organized American Volunteer Group in China (the so-called Flying Tigers) as well as training Chinese pilots in Arizona.[44] The delivery of U.S. military goods to China was hampered not only by other demands on U.S. war production but also by Japan's control of most of China's coastline including all of China's major ports. This left Hong Kong, Burma, and northern French Indochina as the only road and rail conduits for Western military assistance to China. (The airlift of supplies over the Himalayas—"The Hump"—did not begin until July 1942, after the Japanese had seized Hong Kong, Indochina, and the Burma Road.)

Understandably, the Japanese took a dim view of any U.S. or other Western assistance to Chiang Kai-shek. In their diplomatic negotiations with the United States, the Japanese repeatedly insisted that the United States refrain from "interfering" with their attempts to settle what they referred to as the China Incident. Completely ignoring the rising power of Chinese nationalism, which Japan's own behavior in China had done so much to excite, Tokyo regarded the Nationalist Government as illegitimate and believed that Chinese resistance against Japan would cease once China was deprived of external assistance. This placed a premium on halting the flow of military assistance to China; thus for the Japanese, control of Southeast Asia became essential as a means to settling the war in China and to securing the region's vital raw materials.

Nor did the Japanese grasp why the United States cared so much about China. Gordon Prange observed that

> The Japanese never understood why the United States supported China so stubbornly. From a strictly pragmatic view, they could not see why the Americans should care who ruled the Chinese, a nation with which they had no racial, cultural, religious, or political ties. Hence the Japanese imagined that the American was less pro-Chinese than anti-Japanese, part of a plot to whittle their empire down to size and deny to Japan its (to them) rightful and heaven-blessed position as ruler of Asia.[45]

China was much more important to Japan than it was to the United States. In a speech to an America-Japan Society luncheon in December 1940, Japanese Foreign Minister Yosuke Matsuoka declared that "the fate of China is largely a question of sentiment to the Americans, but to us it constitutes a truly vital issue affecting, as it does, the very existence of our Empire."[46] It is not clear that the United States truly comprehended the strength of Tokyo's interest in China or the strategic consequences of the disparity between U.S. and Japanese interests in China. Japan was at war in, with, and for China, whereas every American political administration since McKinley's had made it plain that the United States was not prepared to use force to protect its relatively modest interests in China.

Japan's Alliance with Nazi Germany. On September 27, 1940, in the wake of Hitler's stunning defeat of France and near-defeat of the Royal Air Force in the Battle of Britain, Japan entered a military alliance with Nazi Germany and Fascist Italy. Article 3 of the Tripartite Pact pledged its signatories to "undertake to assist one another with all political, economic and military means when one of the Three Contracting Powers is attacked by a power at present not involved in the European war or in the Chinese-Japanese war." Germany, Italy, and Japan also affirmed that the Pact's terms "do not in any way affect the political status which exists at present between each of the three Contracting Powers and Soviet Russia." (In 1940, relations between Berlin and Moscow were governed by the Infamous Hitler-Stalin Nonaggression Treaty of August 24, 1939, in which Germany and the Soviet Union renounced war against each other and pledged neutrality if the other were attacked by a third party.) Accompanying the Tripartite Pact was a secret exchange of letters between Japanese Foreign Minister Yosuke Matsuoka and Germany's ambassador to Japan, Eugen Ott, in which Japan obtained an escape clause stating that "whether or not a Contracting Party has been attacked within the meaning of Article 3 of the Pact shall be determined through joint consultation among the three Contracting Parties."[47] This proviso, of which the Roosevelt administration knew nothing, essentially permitted Japan, should it so decide, to renege on the defensive military commitment it made to Germany and Italy in Article 3.

Clearly, the Tripartite Pact was directed primarily against the United States, given the strategic collaboration between Nazi Germany and the Soviet Union and the fact that the United States was the only other major power not at war in Europe or Asia. The Pact's intent was to deter the United States from going to war with either Nazi Germany or Japan on pain of going to war with both. Stated Matsuoka, the Pact's main architect, at an Imperial Conference on September 26: "Germany wants to prevent American entry into the war and Japan wants to avoid a war with the United States."[48] Matsuoka told Japanese journalist Masuo Kato that the Pact was "a powerful diplomatic weapon in Japan's hands, a means of bluffing the United States into making the necessary concessions that would lead to a peaceful settlement of disputes in the Pacific."[49] "In effect," observes Robert Divine, "Japan had joined with Germany in an effort to frighten the United States by raising the specter of a two-ocean war."[50] Ambassador Grew concluded at the time, "the primary aim of the pact is the United States, and the German-Italian hope is naturally that the pact will increase American fears of developments in the Pacific."[51] David J. Lu agrees:

The primary objective of the alliance was to eliminate the possibility of American intervention in Europe and Asia. Japan alone was too weak to perform this task, and so was Germany. But the powerful combination of the two would effectively counterbalance the threat posed by the United States. So confident was Matsuoka of the efficacy of the proposed alliance that he even predicted that the Western Hemisphere bloc led by the United States would eventually become a good neighbor of the East Asian Co-Prosperity Sphere.[52]

At a Liaison Conference in mid-September, War Minister Hideki Tojo explained the proposed pact in the context of Japan's war in China: "It is the United States that is encouraging the Chungking Government or anti-Japanese movement at the present time. Should a solid coalition come to exist between Japan, Germany and Italy, it will become the most effectual expedient to restrain the United States. The more effectively we restrain the United States, the more possibly and quickly we shall be able to dispose of the Sino-Japanese conflict."[53] For Hitler and Nazi Foreign Minister Joachim von Ribbentrop, who feared that Roosevelt's increasing assistance to Britain presaged eventual American entry into the war, the Pact's purpose was clear: "to bring Japan into alliance with Germany and Italy in the hope thereby of deterring the United States from active intervention on Britain's behalf. It was greatly in their interest to defeat Britain before the United States threw its weight into the scales," and an alliance with Japan, they hoped, would serve as a "provision against American interference."[54]

The Pact satisfied another major Japanese objective: Germany's recognition of East Asia as Japan's legitimate sphere of influence. In exchange for Japan's recognition of "the leadership of Germany and Italy in the establishment of a new order in Europe," Article 2 of the Pact stated that "Germany and Italy recognize and respect the leadership of Japan in the establishment of a new order in greater East Asia." In the wake of Germany's conquest of France and the Netherlands, and given what appeared to be the imminent defeat of Great Britain, the Japanese worried that Germany might seek to replace the British, French, and

Dutch as the new colonial overlord in Southeast Asia. Though Germany was in no position to project naval power into the region, the Tripartite Pact reassured Tokyo that it would encounter no objections to Japanese expansion into Southeast Asia from Berlin.

The Pact, however, failed in its main purpose—i.e., to intimidate the United States. On the contrary, it "caused a profound hardening of American public opinion toward Japan—a once-and-for-all identification of the Empire with the Axis, with Hitler and the whole program of world conquest and the menace of aggression which America was sure he represented."[55] For years American public opinion had been enraged by Japan's aggression in China, especially by the vividly publicized terror bombings of Chinese cities. Now, as Ambassador Grew observed, Japan had become "part and parcel of that system which, if allowed to develop unchecked, will assuredly destroy everything America stands for."[56] She had become a charter member of the Rome-Berlin-Tokyo Axis bent on conquering the world, and the "automatic effectiveness of the Tripartite Pact . . . was assumed without question."[57] Cordell Hull believed that Germany and Japan were "operating together as any two highwaymen operate and as closely as any two could operate."[58] The fact that the alliance was more appearance than reality, that it was a defensive pact among three states with widely divergent and often conflicting strategic interests and ambitions, was not appreciated until late 1941 and even then only by a small number of U.S. policymakers. As far as American public opinion was concerned, Japan was part of a centrally directed international conspiracy of global conquest. "Japan's formal partnership with Nazi Germany in the Tripartite Alliance was a hard and inescapable fact," observed Hull after the war. "The Japanese had been consistently unwilling in conversations [in 1941] to pledge their Government to renounce Japan's commitments in the alliance. They would not state that Japan would refrain from attacking this country if it [the United States] became involved through self-defense in the European war."[59]

By late 1941 anti-American hardliners in Tokyo recognized that the Tripartite Pact had failed to accomplish its intended purpose. Notwithstanding Japan's alliance with Nazi Germany, the United States had increased aid to Great Britain and Nationalist China, escalated its un-declared naval war against Germany in the North Atlantic, participated in military staff conversations with the British and Dutch in Singapore, and ratcheted up its restrictions on exports to Japan. The Americans were also shipping arms and munitions to the British in Malaya and the Dutch in the Indies. War was an obvious alternative to the failed deterrence of the Tripartite Pact. Even Matsuoka admitted that the Pact was an egregious error. On the day the attack on Pearl Harbor was an-nounced, he declared: "The Tripartite Pact was my worst mistake [as foreign minister]. I hoped to prevent the United States from entering the war. I wanted to adjust our relations with Soviet Russia through this alli-ance. I hoped peace would be maintained and Japan would be placed in a secure position. Instead we see face to face the present calamity which indirectly resulted from the Alliance."[60]

After the war, former ambassador Nomura, who opposed Japan's alliance with Germany, expressed his disbelief that Prime Minister Fu-mimaro Konoye and Matsuoka could believe they could obtain both the alliance and good relations with the United States. "Both Konoye and Matsuoka entertained the fallacy that by means of the Tripartite Alli-ance would Japan be able to extricate herself from her state of isolation and yet at the same time reach an understanding with America," wrote Nomura in 1951. "It is quite astonishing that they should show such a lack of understanding the mentality of the American people."[61]

The situation in September 1940, however, made an alliance with Germany seemingly irresistible. Japan was diplomatically isolated and exhausted by its war in China. In the late summer of 1940, moreover, Ja-pan "had an unshakable belief in the ultimate victory of Germany. From this belief, it followed that Japan needed to align with a victorious pow-er in order to strengthen its international standing and to reach agree-ment with Germany before advancing southward lest Germany claim these regions for itself."[62] In effect, Japan staked its future on Germany's defeat of Great Britain and on the belief that its alliance with Germany could bluff the United States into acquiescence to Tokyo's domination of the Far East.

It is not clear whether Japan's withdrawal from the Tripartite Pact would have thwarted the outbreak of war with the United States. Withdrawal would have satisfied a major U.S. demand and made it difficult for Washington to continue to advance the argument of German-Japanese strategic collusion. There is no reason to believe, however, that withdrawal would have tempered Japanese imperial ambitions in Southeast Asia, which were fundamentally hostile to U.S. interests. The opportunity to withdraw arose in the wake of the German invasion of Russia, which, by driving Moscow into a de facto alliance with Britain and the United States, exposed Japan to the heightened possibility of war with all three countries. The invasion surprised the Japanese as much as it did Stalin and led to the resignation of the second Konoye cabinet. Konoye favored dropping Japan's alliance with Germany, but Matsuoka and the IJA leadership, mesmerized by initial German military successes in Russia, were reluctant to do so. There was also the question of honor: withdrawal would "betray" an ally and could be interpreted as an act of diplomatic capitulation to the United States. Finally, annulment of the Tripartite Pact would enrage younger officers on the IJA General Staff, where pro-Axis sentiment was especially intense, with unpredictable consequences in a country with a recent history of assassination of government leaders by military fanatics.[63]

Japan's Imperial Ambitions in Southeast Asia. On June 29, 1940, in the wake of Germany's conquest of France and the Netherlands, Japanese Foreign Minister Hachiro Arita announced on the radio that Japan's New Order in East Asia (a euphemism for Tokyo's colonial empire) was being extended beyond Korea and China to include *nanyo* ("southern seas")—i.e., Southeast Asia.[64] It was this evident intention to incorporate Southeast Asia into the Japanese Empire that occasioned the outbreak of war between Japan and the United States in December 1941. U.S. economic sanctioning of Japan culminating in the imposition of an oil embargo in July 1941 (see later discussion) persuaded the Japanese leadership, which had long regarded Southeast Asia as properly falling within Japan's natural sphere of influence, that the oil-rich Dutch East Indies had to be seized quickly to offset the loss of American oil. But securing the Indies, the Japanese concluded, also meant eliminating the remaining Western military threat in Southeast Asia, which in turn meant, at a minimum, the seizure of Malaya and the British naval base at Singapore.

For the Roosevelt administration, a Japanese conquest of Southeast Asia, even if it bypassed the Philippines, was unacceptable. In the administration's view, Japan's seizure of the oil, tin, rubber, and other resources of Southeast Asia would strengthen Japan's economic base, deprive Great Britain of resources essential to her continued prosecution of the war in Europe, and threaten Australia, New Zealand, and India, which together supplied much of the British Empire's military manpower. In January 1941 Roosevelt wrote Ambassador Grew that "we must consider whether if Japan should gain possession of the region of the Netherlands East Indies and the Malay Peninsula, the chances of England's winning in her struggle with Germany would not be decreased thereby." In Roosevelt's view, the British Isles "have been able to exist and to defend themselves not only because they have prepared strong local defenses but also because as the heart and nerve center of the British Empire they have been able to draw [on] the vast resources for their sustenance and to bring into operation against their enemies economic, military, and naval pressures on a worldwide scale."[65] The previous September, Grew had cabled the State Department, "If [U.S.] support to the British Empire in this hour of her travail is conceived to be in our interest, and most emphatically do I so conceive it, we must strive by every means to preserve the *status quo* in the Pacific, at least until the war in Europe has been won or lost."[66]

In February 1941 Eugene Dooman, counselor of the U.S. embassy in Tokyo, forcefully linked Southeast Asia's fate to the war in Europe to Japanese Vice Foreign Minister Chuichi Ohashi:

[A]n adequate supply of airplanes and other munitions [by the United States] is not the only prerequisite to a British victory; the supply to England of foodstuffs and raw materials by the British dominions and colonies and the maintenance of British commerce with the outside world are equally essential to a British victory. It would be absurd to suppose that the American people, while pouring munitions into Britain, would look with complacency upon the cutting of communications between Britain and British dominions and colonies overseas. If, therefore, Japan or any other nation were to prejudice the safety of those communications, she would have to expect to come into conflict with the United States. There are many indications of the Japanese moving slowly toward Singapore and the Netherlands East Indies. . . . [I]f Japan were to occupy these strategically important British and Dutch areas, it could easily debouch into the Indian Ocean and the South Pacific and create havoc with essential British lines of communication. . . . However greatly Japan's security might be enhanced by occupying the Netherlands East Indies it must be realized by Japan that any such move would vitally concern the major preoccupation of the United States at this time, which is to assist England to stand against German assault.[67]

Three months later, Grew reiterated the U.S. position to Foreign Minister Matsuoka, telling him that it "would be utter folly for us, having adopted a policy of supporting Great Britain, to supply Great Britain by the Atlantic while complacently watching the downfall of Britain through the severance of the British lifeline from the East."[68]

Japanese intentions in Southeast Asia were certainly no secret. Incorporation of the region into Japan's Greater East Asia Co-Prosperity Sphere—a euphemism for territorial empire—was openly discussed in Tokyo and covertly encrypted in Japanese cable traffic. For example, an intercepted dispatch from Tokyo to Japanese military attachés on July 14, 1941, stated that "After the occupation of Indochina, next on our schedule is the sending of an ultimatum to the Netherlands Indies. In the seizing of Singapore the Navy will play the principal part. As for the Army, in seizing Singapore it will need only one division and in seizing the Netherlands Indies, only two."[69]

Thus for the United States, what counted most was the effect of a Japanese move into Southeast Asia not on the West's position in the Far East, but on Britain's war against Hitler in Europe. Given the fact that by the fall of 1941 the United States had dropped any pretense of neutrality in Britain's war against Nazi Germany and was providing military sup-

plies to Britain while simultaneously attacking on sight German submarines in the North Atlantic, a Japanese attack on the British in Southeast Asia could be interpreted as tantamount to a vicarious attack on
America's tacit ally. Whether the United States and Great Britain were
strategically inseparable in the fall of 1941 to the point that the United
States would fight even in the event of a Japanese invasion of Southeast
Asia that did not involve attacks on American territory or U.S. naval
forces is an issue that will be addressed later. Suffice to say here that
the Japanese initially wrestled with this issue but finally concluded that
the United States would forcibly respond to a Japanese attack on British
possessions in Southeast Asia. The Japanese believed that the Anglo-
Saxon powers and the Dutch were acting in concert with each other and
that they would collectively defend Western interests in Southeast Asia.
If America was supporting Great Britain in Europe, it would also support the British in the Far East.

Japanese intentions in Southeast Asia were confirmed when Japan,
under the provisions of an agreement coerced from the Vichy regime
in unoccupied France on July 21, 1941, proceeded to occupy southern
Indochina with 50,000 troops, taking over from the French eight air-
fields and two naval bases (at Cam Ranh and Saigon). Japan was thus
positioned, with its land-based air power now within range, to threaten
Malaya, the Dutch East Indies, and the Philippines.[70] As Acting Secretary of State Sumner Welles stated to the Japanese ambassador, Admiral
Nomura, on July 23:

> The movement now undertaken by Japan could only be regarded
> by the United States as having two purposes, neither of which pur-
> poses this Government could ignore: First, the United States could
> only assume that the occupation of Indo-China by Japan consti-
> tuted notice to the United States that the Japanese Government in-
> tended to pursue a policy of force and conquest, and second, that
> in the light of these acts on the part of Japan, the United States,
> with regard to its own safety in the light of its own preparations
> for self-defense, must assume that the Japanese Government was
> taking the last step before proceeding upon a policy of totalitarian

expansion in the South Seas through the seizure of additional territories in that region.[71]

The following day Welles issued a public statement that Japan's occupation of southern Indochina was "undertaken because of the estimated value to Japan of bases in that region primarily for purposes of further and more obvious movements on conquest in adjacent areas."[72]

U.S. Embargoes on Japanese Trade. In his history of U.S.-Japanese relations, Walter LaFeber writes that the years 1937–1941 "not only vividly demonstrated Japan's dependence on [its] relationship [with the United States], but how each time Japan tried to use its diplomacy or military force to break that dependence, the dependence only tightened." The relationship "resembled a slip knot in which the more Japan struggled against it, the tighter it became—until, finally, the Japanese Empire strangled."[73] In July 1939, two months before the outbreak of war in Europe, the United States informed Japan that it intended to abrogate the 1911 U.S.-Japan Treaty of Commerce and Navigation at the end of the required six-month notice (January 1940). The treaty essentially granted Japan economic access on a most-favored-nation basis. Coming on the heels of Japan's continued aggression in China and increasing alignment with Nazi Germany, the meaning of the abrogation was clear: from here on out the Roosevelt administration was prepared to employ Tokyo's enormous trade dependence on the United States as a weapon to deter further Japanese foreign policy transgressions. As Secretary of State Cordell Hull noted at the time, "How can we treat Japan as a friendly nation when its whole policy is hostile to American interests?"[74] After the war, Hull recalled that "It was felt that this treaty was not affording adequate protection to American commerce either in Japan or in the Japanese occupied portions of China, while at the same time the operation of the most-favored nation clause of the treaty was a bar to the adoption of retaliatory measures against Japanese commerce."[75] Less than a month before the treaty expired, Grew declared that "More than anything else the termination of the Treaty of Commerce and Navigation casts the darkest shadow over American-Japanese relations."[76] Clearly, notes Roosevelt biographer H. W. Brands, the "president's purpose [in not renewing the treaty] was to remind the Japanese of their dependence on the United States for vital raw materials, including oil and scrap iron and steel."[77] Over the next eighteen months, the United States embargoed an ever-growing number of U.S. exports, culminating in July 1941 in a freezing of all Japanese assets in the United States that effectively halted U.S. trade with Japan, including the continued shipment of oil upon which the Japanese economy and war machine were critically dependent.[78]

Economic sanctions served as a substitute for the armed force the Roosevelt administration was never prepared to use on behalf of China and other victims of Japanese aggression in East Asia. Though the administration recognized Chiang Kai-shek's Kuomintang as the legitimate government of China and provided it financial and later, military assistance, it never even threatened to go to war with Japan over Tokyo's aggression in China. On the contrary, the administration in 1939–1941 was fixated on the Nazi German threat in Europe, especially after the fall of France in the summer of 1940. Roosevelt and the U.S. military leadership rightly regarded Germany as a much greater threat to core American security interests than Japan. No one in the administration wanted a war in the Pacific at a time when Great Britain's, and later the Soviet Union's, survival seemed at stake. Given these circumstances, economic sanctions seemed to offer an effective means of containing Japanese imperial ambitions in East Asia without recourse to war.

A policy of sanctions for the purpose of deterrence, however, rested on the assumption that because Japan knew it could not win a war with the United States, it would respond to sanctions by altering its foreign policies in directions favorable to the United States. Understandably— and legitimately—the Japanese regarded the steadily rising U.S. trade restrictions as hostile acts intended to coerce Japan into submission, and they recognized that Japan's extraordinary dependence on imported American oil and other items critical to her industrial base and military forces placed the United States in a position to strangle Japan's economy, and by extension her ability to fight.

In retrospect, the Pacific War of 1941–1945 seems inevitable, given the scope of Japan's imperial ambitions, her reckless pursuit of them, and the U.S. refusal to accept Japan's control of Southeast Asia. To argue that the war was historically determined, however, is to claim that Japanese and American political and military leaders had no control over events—that they were simply bowling pins at the mercy of the laws of physics. This is simply not the case. They may have misjudged and miscalculated, ignored unpleasant facts, and engaged in wishful thinking, but they consciously made decisions, and those decisions had consequences, intended or otherwise. Roosevelt most assuredly did not want war in the Pacific, at least not until the war in Europe had been decided, and he and Hull worked tirelessly to avoid it. Nor was Japan destined to attack the United States; she could have chosen, as she did briefly in the 1920s and for good in the postwar decades, to accept trade dependence on the United States in the context of a liberal political and economic order.

CHAPTER THREE

Japanese Aggression and U.S. Policy Responses, 1937–1941

The Japanese decision for war against the United States was the product of offended honor, fatalism, racial arrogance, cultural incomprehension, economic desperation, and strategic miscalculation. "Japan's long-range dreams of expansion, of access to raw materials to relieve the pressure of population, underlay a complex combination of diplomatic, political, and military miscalculations that led the country to war when peace might have been possible," observed Masuo Kato in 1946. "German influence, the preoccupation [with] Russia, racial antipathies, fear and distrust of the Western powers, the personal ambitions of Japan's leaders, the insistence of the military upon regaining the face that had been lost in the ill-conceived, ill-executed China incident all played a part in leading to the superficial events that caused the war."[1]

The decision followed four years of stalemated Japanese aggression in China, Tokyo's proclamation in August 1940 of a "Greater East Asian Co-Prosperity Sphere" that encompassed Southeast Asia as well as China, Manchuria, and Korea, and Japan's entry into a military alliance—the Tripartite Pact of September 1940—with Nazi Germany and Fascist Italy. Having annexed Korea in 1910 and seized Manchuria in 1931, Japan invaded China in 1937. By the beginning of 1941 Japan had conquered much of north and central China, seized all of China's major ports as well as Hainan Island and the Spratly Islands in the South China Sea, and established a military presence in northern French Indochina. Japan was poised to invade resource-rich Southeast Asia, which

Japanese propagandists had long and loudly proclaimed to be rightfully within Japan's sphere of influence, notwithstanding the fact that almost all of Southeast Asia lay under British, Dutch, French, and American colonial rule.

The United States had never recognized Japan's Manchurian puppet state of Manchukuo and opposed Japan's war in China. The United States recognized Chiang Kai-shek's Kuomintang as the legitimate government of China and provided it financial and military assistance. The Roosevelt administration also rightly regarded the Tripartite Pact as directed against the United States. Japan's alliance with Hitler, which was clearly intended to deter the United States from going to war with Germany or Japan by raising the specter of a two-ocean war,[2] transformed Japan from regional threat into a potential extension of Hitler's agenda of aggression, especially with respect to the Soviet Union after the Nazi invasion of June 22, 1941. "No other action could so directly or effectively have seemed to bear out the contention of the hardline faction in Washington that Japan's southward drive was part of a vast Axis plan for world conquest that would eventually reach America unless she acted immediately to stop it," observes Sachiko Murakami.[3] Roosevelt viewed the Soviet Union as an indispensable belligerent against Hitler and took the threat of a Japanese invasion of Siberia from Manchuria quite seriously. There is even evidence that he deliberately stiffened U.S. policy toward Japan in the wake of Germany's invasion of Russia for the purpose of encouraging the Japanese to look south rather than north.[4] "The great question for world leaders in the first half of 1941 was whether Hitler would attack the Soviet Union, and the great question in the latter half was whether he would succeed," observes Waldo Heinrichs. "The German-Soviet conflict had a direct bearing on Japanese-American relations."[5]

There is no doubt that U.S. policy toward Japan hardened in mid-1941. In May, Roosevelt declared China eligible for Lend-Lease assistance, raising the prospect of more effective Chinese resistance against the Japanese. Two months later came the administration's decisions to freeze Japanese assets in the United States and to reinforce the Philippines. Roosevelt apparently believed that the diversion of so much of

Nazi Germany's military might into the Soviet Union lessened the German threat to Great Britain, and in so doing enabled the United States to take a stronger stand in the Pacific, and "[t]his conviction, shared by Stimson and others, was a basic factor in the decisions made during the months before Pearl Harbor."[6]

Another basic factor, as we have seen, was that the Roosevelt administration viewed a Japanese invasion of Southeast Asia, especially the oil-rich Dutch East Indies and tin- and rubber-rich British Malaya, as strategically unacceptable. Control of Southeast Asia would not only weaken the British Empire and threaten India, Australia, and New Zealand, it would also afford Japan access to oil and other critical raw materials that would reduce its economic dependence on the United States. The administration, contends Jonathan Marshall, was wedded to the "fundamental proposition that the United States and Britain could not afford to lose the raw material wealth and the sea lanes of Southeast Asia" even if it meant war.[7] Though the administration was not prepared to go to war over China, it regarded an extension of Japan's empire into Southeast Asia as a war-threatening act. Thus Japan provoked a strong American response when Japanese forces occupied *southern* French Indochina in July 1941 as an obvious preliminary to further southward military moves. (In 1940 the United States had cracked Japan's most secret diplomatic code—known as PURPLE—and was therefore privy to key foreign ministry traffic regarding Japan's intentions.) As a post–Pearl Harbor State Department memorandum concluded:

By this further expansion in southern Indochina Japan virtually completed the encirclement of the Philippine Islands and placed its armed forces within striking distance of vital trade routes. This constituted an overt act directly menacing the security of the United States. . . . It created a situation in which the risk of war became so great that the United States and other countries concerned were confronted no longer with the question of avoiding such risk but from then on with the problem of preventing a complete undermining of their security. . . . With Japan's armed forces poised for further attacks, the possibility of averting armed conflict lay only in the bare chance that there might be reached some agreement which would cause Japan to abandon her policy . . . of aggression. Under those circumstances and in light of those considerations, the Government of the United States decided at that point . . . that discontinuance of trade with Japan had become an appropriate and necessary step—as an open warning to Japan and as a measure of self-defense.[8]

In December 1940, Grew had warned Roosevelt from Tokyo that

Only insuperable obstacles will now prevent the Japanese from digging in permanently in China and from pushing the southward advance with economic control as preliminary to political domination in the areas marked down. Economic obstacles, such as may arise from American embargoes, will seriously handicap Japan in the long run, but meanwhile they tend to push the Japanese onward in a forlorn hope of making themselves economically self-sufficient.[9]

The United States nonetheless declared total economic war on Japan in July 1941 as a means of deterring—or at least delaying—a Japanese advance into Southeast Asia. Significantly, Roosevelt did not envisage an abrupt shutdown of all U.S. trade with Japan when he signed the order freezing Japanese assets in the United States on July 26. As Roosevelt told Secretary of the Interior Harold Ickes, he intended to use the order's requirement that the Japanese obtain export licenses to release frozen dollars for purchase of any further U.S. products as a "noose around Japan's neck" which he would "jerk now and then."[10] The aim of the asset freeze, at least in Roosevelt's mind, "was to avoid provoking Japan while bringing more and more pressure to bear, not only to impede Japan's war production, but also to haunt it with the constant threat that more severe measures might be applied."[11] As William Langer and Everett Gleason observed in their seminal 1953 work, *The Undeclared War 1940–1941: The World Crisis and American Foreign Policy,* "In effect what Roosevelt decided to do was to emit a loud and resounding bark, in the hope that Tokyo might yet be frightened away from its prey. If this proved futile, he proposed to bite, as often and hard as the situation might require."[12] Thus Roosevelt intended that oil shipments to Japan continue, albeit in reduced quantities, because he believed that a complete embargo could provoke a Japanese attack on the Dutch East Indies.[13] The Roosevelt administration was well aware that Japan imported 90 percent of its oil, 75 to 80 percent of which was from the United States (which in 1940 accounted for an astounding 63 percent of the world's output of petroleum). Roosevelt also knew that the Dutch East Indies, which produced 3 percent of the world's output, was the only other convenient oil producer that could meet Japan's import needs.[14]

The freeze order was the culmination of a program of sanctioning Japan for its aggression in China that began in January 1940 with the U.S. withdrawal from its 1911 commercial treaty with Japan (notice of abrogation was given in July 1939). As early as 1937, Roosevelt had toyed with the idea of strangling Japan's trade via a distant Anglo-American naval "quarantine" of Japan in which the U.S. Navy would blockade Japan from the Aleutian Islands to Hawaii and the Royal Navy would blockade from Hawaii to Singapore.[15] A cooperative Royal Navy was, of course, an impossibility as long as Neville Chamberlain remained Britain's prime minister. The abrogation of the U.S.-Japanese Commercial Treaty, however, cleared the deck for unilateral American action. Indeed, sanctioning escalated in July 1940 with the passage of the National Defense Act, which granted the administration authority to ban or restrict the export of items declared vital to national defense. On July 25, Roosevelt announced a ban on Japanese acquisition of U.S. high-octane aviation gasoline, certain grades of steel and scrap iron, and some lubricants. In September the White House imposed a ban on all scrap iron exports to Japan. Because the Japanese steel industry was highly dependent on imported scrap iron from the United States, the ban compelled Japan to draw down its stockpiles and operate its steel industry well below capacity; indeed, the ban blocked any significant expansion of Japanese steel production during the war.[16] In December the embargo was expanded to include iron ore, steel, and steel products, and in the following month, copper (of which the United States supplied 80 percent of Japan's requirements), brass, bronze, zinc, nickel, and potash. "Almost every week thereafter other items were added to the list, each of which was much needed for Japanese industrial production."[17] Thus by July 1941, the United States was seriously punishing Japan for its continued aggression in China and adherence to the Tripartite Pact.

By early 1941 the United States had in place an imposing number of embargoes on the shipment of materials to Japan, nearly all of them had been justified—most of them correctly—as measures necessary for the American rearmament effort. But for this very reason they had a substantial impact on Japan's own war economy. Tokyo's only source of materials crucial for war—scrap iron, steel, machine tools, ferroalloys, aluminum—was, excepting a trickle of supplies from Germany that came over the trans-Siberian railroad, the United States.[18]

But, as Roosevelt understood, it was Japan's oil dependency on the United States, a dependency, ironically, that had deepened with Japan's expanding military operations in China, that constituted the real hangman's noose around Japan's neck. Moreover, by the summer of 1941 it had become politically difficult for the Roosevelt administration to justify the continued shipment of a commodity on which the Japanese war machine was so dependent. American public opinion was increasingly outraged, as were key members of Roosevelt's cabinet, including Secretary of the Interior Harold Ickes, Secretary of the Treasury Henry Morgenthau, Secretary of the Navy Frank Knox, and Secretary of War Henry Stimson, all of whom believed that the continued shipment of oil to Japan was a national disgrace.[19] (Ickes favored a preventive war against Japan,[20] and Stimson, before joining the Roosevelt administration, had headed the American Committee for Non-Participation in Japanese Aggression.) Thus for State and Treasury department hardliners "who saw Japan as the enemy and economic sanctions as the effective weapon at hand," a limited oil embargo was a half-measure positively begging for bureaucratic sabotage.[21] Led by State Department hawks Acheson and Stanley Hornbeck, head of State's Far Eastern Division, they believed Japan was a paper tiger that would collapse in response to strong U.S. pressure. They were determined to threaten Japan's economic ruin by converting the freeze order into a complete suspension of trade (including oil) through their control of the complicated procedures that compelled Japanese importers to obtain export licenses from the State Department as well as exchange permits (to release frozen funds) from the Treasury Department.[22] Both Acheson and Morgenthau had favored punitive sanctions for years and took advantage of the freeze order to deny all Japanese requests for licenses and exchange permits.[23]

The result, in conjunction with the U.S.-encouraged seizure of Japanese assets by Great Britain and the Netherlands, was a complete suspension of Japanese economic access to the United States and the destruction of between 50 and 75 percent of Japan's foreign trade.[24] In early November 1941, Joseph Grew cabled Hull that "the greater part of Japanese commerce has been lost, Japanese industrial production has been drastically curtailed, and Japan's national resources have been depleted." Grew went on to warn of "an all-out, do-or-die attempt, actually risking national hara-kiri, to make Japan impervious to economic embargoes abroad rather than to yield to foreign pressure."[25] Even in retrospect, Acheson, for his part, claimed that the embargo's aim was "to limit Japanese military action in East and Southeast Asia," and that though the "danger of provoking Japan to seize . . . the Dutch East Indies . . . or move against us" was recognized, the feeling was that "no rational Japanese could believe that an attack on us could result in anything but disaster for his country. Of course, no one even dimly foresaw the initial success of [the Japanese] attack [on Pearl Harbor]."[26]

Roosevelt was much less confident. Neither he nor U.S. Army Chief of Staff George Marshall nor U.S. Chief of Naval Operations Harold "Betty" Stark wanted to force a showdown with Japan. All three men were preoccupied with the war in Europe and regarded Nazi Germany as a far greater threat to U.S. security than Imperial Japan. Marshall, Stark, and other senior U.S. military leaders favored restraint in the Pacific, and wanted time to shore up U.S. defenses in the Philippines.[27] Roosevelt wanted the bargaining leverage of a limited embargo because he believed that an abrupt shutdown of U.S. trade with Japan would likely provoke a Japanese advance into Southeast Asia, which would probably mean war. As early as October 1940 Roosevelt told Hull and

Under-Secretary of State Sumner Welles that an oil shut-off would force Japan to attack the Dutch East Indies, a judgment he repeated to a White House audience just two days after ordering the freezing of Japanese assets.[28] On July 24, 1941, according to Welles, Roosevelt told the Japanese ambassador that

> for more than two years the United States had been permitting oil to be exported from the United States to Japan. He said that this had been done because of the realization on the part of the United States that if these oil supplies had been shut off or restricted the Japanese Government and people would have been furnished with an incentive or a pretext for moving down upon the Netherlands East Indies in order to assure themselves of a greater oil supply than that which, under present conditions, they were able to obtain. . . . The President . . . went on to say that this new move by Japan in Indochina created an exceedingly serious problem for the United States. [29]

The next day Roosevelt told a group of civil defense enthusiasts that "there was—you might call—a method in letting this oil go to Japan, with the hope—and it has worked for two years—of keeping war out of the South Pacific for our own good, for the good of the defense of Great Britain, and the freedom of the seas."[30]

Yet upon discovering, after his return from the Placentia Bay conference with Winston Churchill in August, that all oil exports to Japan had, in fact, been suspended, Roosevelt declined to reverse the decision. The reasons remain unclear. Perhaps he believed that a reversal would look like a retreat—a sign of weakness to the Japanese, or perhaps he had come to regard a Japanese advance into Southeast Asia as inevitable. If war were now a certainty, then a complete embargo would at least weaken Japan's capacity to wage war.[31] Roosevelt was also pursuing a highly interventionist policy in Europe for which he needed the support of Stimson, Morgenthau, Ickes, and other anti-Japanese hardliners; he may have felt that he risked alienating the hardliners by continued lack of decisive intervention against Japan.[32]

There was also the issue of public opinion, which since 1937 had increasingly favored tough economic sanctions against Japan. Indeed, public opinion on sanctions ran well ahead of Roosevelt and the cautious Cordell Hull.[33] In the summer of 1938 the American Committee for Non-Participation in Japanese Aggression was formed with then private citizen Henry Stimson serving as honorary chairman.[34] The committee eventually attracted almost three thousand financial contributors and a distinguished list of sponsors. By the summer of 1939 strong majorities of Americans favored embargoing arms and ammunition, and by October 1940, in the wake of the formation of the Axis alliance, some 83 percent supported embargoing the sale of all war goods, including oil and gasoline.[35] In the summer of 1941, for Roosevelt to have backed away from the complete trade shutdown engineered by anti-Japanese hawks within the State and Treasury departments would have invited an avalanche of public condemnation.

The culmination of U.S. economic warfare against Japan in the summer of 1941 confronted Tokyo with essentially two choices: seize Southeast Asia or submit to the United States. Economic destitution and attendant military paralysis would soon become a reality if Japan did nothing. Less than a week after the embargo's imposition, the Japanese Foreign Ministry cabled the Japanese ambassador to Germany: "Commercial and economic relations between Japan and other countries, led by England and the United States, are gradually becoming so horribly strained that we cannot endure it much longer. Consequently, the Japanese Empire, to save its very life, must take measures to secure the raw materials of the South Seas."[36] By late summer the embargo was beginning to strangle Japanese industry, and Japan's stockpiled oil amounted to no more than eighteen to twenty-four months of normal consumption —and substantially less should Japan mount major military operations in Southeast Asia.[37] As National Planning Board director Teiichi Suzuki declared before an Imperial audience on September 6, 1941:

> At this stage our national power with respect to physical resources has come to depend entirely upon the productive capacity of the Empire itself, upon that of Manchuria, China, Indochina . . . and

upon vital materials stockpiled so far. Therefore, as a result of the present overall economic blockade imposed by Great Britain and the United States, our Empire's national power is declining day by day. Our liquid fuel stockpile, which is the most important, will reach bottom by June or July of next year, even if we impose strict wartime control on civilian demand. Accordingly, I believe it is vitally important for the survival of our Empire that we make up our minds to establish and stabilize a firm economic base. [38]

Two months later, at another conference of Japanese leaders, Prime Minister Hideki Tojo warned that "Two years from now we will have no petroleum for military use. Ships will stop moving." [39]

Yet the price the Americans demanded for lifting the embargo and restoring U.S.-Japanese trade to some semblance of normality was no more acceptable: abandonment of empire. The Roosevelt administration demanded that Japan not only terminate its membership in the Tripartite Alliance but also withdraw its military forces from both China and Indochina, and by extension, the Japanese feared, Manchuria (after all, the United States had refused to recognize the Japanese puppet state of Manchukuo). Abandonment of China and Indochina would have compelled Japan to write off its hard-won gains on the Asian mainland since 1937 and abandon any hope of becoming the dominant power in East Asia. For Japan, a major reason for establishing an empire in East Asia was to free itself of the very kind of humiliating economic dependency on the United States that the embargo represented. And what was to stop the Americans from coercing further territorial concessions from the Japanese, including withdrawal from Manchuria and even Korea and Formosa? Japan "could not accept any interim solution that left it dependent on American largesse" or any deal that left it in a position of "continued reliance on the whims of Washington. The possibility that the Americans might supply Japan with just enough oil, steel, and other materials to maintain a starveling existence was intolerable to any Japanese statesman." [40] Consider the assessment of Yoshimichi Hara, president of the Imperial Privy Council (composed of Japan's ex-premiers), on the eve of the Pearl Harbor attack:

If we were to give in, we would give up in one stroke not only our gains in the Sino-Japanese and Russo-Japanese wars, but also the benefits of the Manchurian Incident. This we cannot do. We are loath to compel our people to suffer even greater hardships, on top of what they have endured during the four years since the China Incident. But it is clear that the existence of our country is being threatened, that the great achievements of the Emperor Meiji would all come to naught, and that there is nothing else we can do. [41]

For Tojo, the choice was between "glory or oblivion." [42] As for the U.S. demand that Japan evacuate China:

withdrawal of our troops [would be] retreat. We sent a large force of one million men [to China], and it has cost us well over 100,000 dead and wounded, [the grief of] their bereaved families, hardship for four years, and a national expenditure of several tens of billions of yen. We must by all means get satisfactory results from this. If we should withdraw troops stationed in China . . . China would become worse than she was before the China Incident. She would even attempt to rule Manchuria, Korea, and Formosa. . . . [T]he stationing of troops [in China] that Japan insists upon is not at all unreasonable. [43]

The United States was, in effect, demanding that Japan renounce its status as an aspiring great power and consign itself to permanent strategic dependency on a hostile America. Such a choice would have been unacceptable to any great power. Japan's survival as a major industrial and military power was at stake—far more compelling reasons for war, one might observe, than the United States later advanced for its disastrous wars of choice in Vietnam and Iraq. Would the United States ever have permitted a hostile power to wreck its foreign commerce and strangle its domestic economy without a resort to war?

If the United States had been faced with a similar boycott which equally endangered its future, few Americans would have ques-

tioned the propriety of waging a major war to restore the prereq-
uisites of American survival. . . . A body blow of this caliber could
have driven multitudes beyond even caring about "winability."
National self-respect and even the quest for naked vengeance . . .
would have reinforced necessity and swept aside any objections.
If the United States would have launched a preemptive war under such circumstances, why is it so surprising that the Japanese
did so?[44]

The American campaign of economic warfare culminating in the total embargo of U.S. trade with Japan in the late summer of 1941 made
sense only as a defense measure—i.e., as a means of weakening Japan in
anticipation of inevitable war. It had little chance of success as a deterrent to war because the Japanese, with considerable reason, regarded
the embargo as an act of war mandating a response in kind.

Roberta Wohlstetter contended that, for Japan, "war with the United States was not chosen. The decision for war was rather forced by the
desire to avoid the terrible alternative of losing status or abandoning
[its] national objectives."[45] The historian Akira Iriye has written of the
oil embargo that it

> had a tremendous psychological impact upon the Japanese. The
> ambivalence and ambiguities in their perception of world events
> disappeared, replaced by a sense of clear-cut alternatives. Hitherto
> they had not confronted the stark choice between war and peace
> as an immediate prospect and had lived in a climate of uncertainty
> from day to day. Now, with the United States resorting to decisive
> measures, that phase passed. Any wishful thinking that America
> would tolerate the invasion of southern Indochina was dissipat-
> ed; either Japan would stay in Southeast Asia at the risk of war
> with the Anglo-American countries or it would retreat to conciliate
> them. The military judged that it was too late for conciliation; Japan
> would now have to consider the likelihood of war, with the United
> States as its major adversary.[46]

Ian Kershaw contends that "For no faction of the Japanese elites could there be a retreat from the goals of a victorious settlement in China and successful expansion to establish . . . Japanese domination of the Far East." These objectives "had not just become an economic imperative. They reflected honour and national pride, the prestige and standing of a great power. The alternatives were seen as not just poverty, but defeat, humiliation, ignominy and an end to great power status in permanent subordination to the United States."[47] Indeed, better to die fighting than to capitulate. "[S]ince Japan is unavoidably facing national ruin whether it decides to fight the United States or submit to its demands, it must by all means choose to fight," declared Admiral Osami Nagano, the chief of staff of the Imperial Japanese Navy, at an Imperial Conference in September 1941. "Japan would rather go down fighting than ignobly surrender without a struggle because surrender would spell spiritual as well as physical ruin for the nation and its destiny."[48] Shortly after Pearl Harbor, George H. E. Smith, an American expert on U.S.-Japanese relations, expressed the judgment, which must have been poorly received by many of his fellow citizens, that

To meet the American position, Japan would have had to retire from China, respect the territory and political independence of Asian countries, subscribe to the Open Door policy, agree to conduct her relations according to law, order, and peaceful measures, relinquish her claim to domination over the "Greater East Asia Co-Prosperity Sphere," and withdraw from her association with the Axis powers. However just and equitable this may have been from an American viewpoint—considering the United States was willing to take measures to ease Japan's economic strain—it was too much to expect from Japan at this juncture. It asked her to reverse half a century of Japanese policy at a single stroke, to give up all that had been gained in China since 1931, and to cast about once more for some solution to her growing population and needs for raw materials. Given time, remedies might have been found, as they will have to be after the present war is over, but that was hardly possible in the atmosphere that prevailed in the first week in December, 1941.[49]

It is doubtful that war could have been avoided even had the United States dropped its insistence that Japan quit China and the Tripartite Pact. Long before Roosevelt froze Japanese assets, the IJN, anticipating the probability of U.S. sanctions in the form of embargoed access to American oil, looked to the Dutch East Indies as the only suitable alternative source. The Japanese navy, which by one estimate accounted for a staggering 60 percent of Japan's total petroleum consumption during the Pacific War,[50] provided the link between the Dutch East Indies and the inevitability of war with the United States. David Evans and Mark Peattie, in their definitive *Kaigun: Strategy, Tactics, and Technology in the Imperial Japanese Navy 1887–1941*, describe the "circular chain of navy reasoning" that made war with the United States a self-fulfilling prophecy:

> In the worsening climate of Japan-U.S. relations, so the line of argument went, the United States would most probably reduce or entirely ban its export of oil to Japan. Since the United States had supplied the navy with most of its petroleum needs, the navy would be obliged to look to the Netherlands East Indies. But to take the oil fields of the Indies by force would embroil Japan in a war with the United States, which Japan could not possibly win without access to those very same sources. Very little evidence suggests that the Japanese naval leadership ever questioned the circularity of the argument by seeking policy alternatives that might have made it less necessary to consider war with the United States.[51]

War—even a lost war—was clearly preferable to humiliation and starvation. Seizure of the Dutch East Indies and British possessions in Southeast Asia (Malaya, Singapore, Sarawak, Brunei, and British North Borneo) offered Japan the only alternative to oil and other resource dependence on the United States. It also meant certain war with Great Britain and the Netherlands, and probable war with the United States.

Neither the British nor the Dutch were in a position to defend their Southeast Asian possessions, however, and the United States was preoccupied with events in Europe.

Could the Japanese move into Southeast Asia without provoking war with the United States? Japanese leaders were initially divided on this question, but finally concluded that even a southward military advance that avoided attacks on the Philippines and other American targets almost certainly would provoke an armed U.S. response, and therefore that it was imperative to strike the first blow. Even if Japan's advance did not provoke war, an untouched Philippines (and U.S. Pacific Fleet at Pearl Harbor) would constitute an unacceptable potential military threat along the eastern flank of Japan's southward advance. IJN leaders were particularly insistent that the United States and Great Britain were strategically inseparable and that Washington would go to war with Japan if Japan went to war with Great Britain.[52] "The Japanese Navy always tended to think that if Japan attacked Singapore or the [Dutch East] Indies the American Navy would sooner or later enter the war," observed Herbert Feis in 1950. "But it was hardly less bothered by the thought that we would keep the main Pacific fleet out of the Southwestern Pacific, until we could use it tellingly in a flank attack."[53] Hawaiian-based U.S. naval power also could threaten the Japanese home islands—as the famous Doolittle raid of carrier-launched B-25 medium bombers against Tokyo demonstrated just four months after the Japanese attack on Pearl Harbor. Indeed, the raid, though causing little damage, revealed the bankruptcy of Japanese strategy: possession of Southeast Asia and most of the Asian mainland counted for little against an enemy capable of striking Japan itself—or, to put it another way, the raid exposed the folly of attempting to wage a limited war against an enemy capable and, after Pearl Harbor, eager to wage total war. Bureaucratic considerations were also powerfully present: an advance into Southeast Asia that did not provoke war with the United States would condemn the IJN to perpetual strategic and budgetary inferiority to the Japanese army. Avoidance of war with the United States "meant that the navy, which for decades had justified its existence by an American naval threat, would have only a very minor role in a Southeast Asian campaign," observe Evans and Peattie. Moreover, "by accepting such a role, the navy could hardly lay claim to the greater allocation of strategic materials required for its major expansion plans."[54]

Additionally, by this time many Japanese leaders had come to believe that war with the United States was inevitable, and there seemed to be no appreciation of the difficulties Roosevelt would have confronted in securing a congressional declaration of war in response to a Japanese attack only on British and Dutch colonial possessions in Southeast Asia.

> By the end of the 1930s [Japan's] international intransigence and naked military aggression had created a situation in which the survival of Japan as a great power, and of her conception of an Asian empire, did indeed hang in the balance. By the fall of 1941 the question had come to be not whether there was to be a war with the Western powers, including the latently powerful United States, but, given the regional and world situation, whether there would ever come a more favorable time to solve Japan's resource problems by military action.[55]

The freezing of Japanese assets in the United States made a U.S-Japanese war unavoidable absent a Japanese capitulation to American diplomatic demands or a profound policy reversal by the Roosevelt administration. And once war is regarded as inevitable, the temptation to initiate it can become irresistible. Time was certainly not on Japan's side; American rearmament would eventually tip the military scales hopelessly against Tokyo.

That said, even if war with the United States was inevitable by, say, September 1941, the Japanese might have profited more by luring the Europe-focused and isolationism-bedeviled Roosevelt administration into firing the first shot. "Perhaps the major Japanese error was their decision to attack the United States at all," speculates Louis Morton. "Their strategic objectives lay in Southeast Asia and if they had limited their attacks to British and Dutch territory the United States might never have entered the war. Such a course would have involved risk, but it would have forced the United States to act first" in the face of "strong opposition to a move that would have appeared to a large part of the American people as an effort to pull British and Dutch chestnuts out of the fire." Instead, "the Japanese relieved the United States government from the necessity of making a very difficult choice."[56] The advantages of allowing the Japanese to start the war were certainly not lost on Roosevelt or Stimson, who discussed the issue at a cabinet meeting two weeks before Pearl Harbor. "If you know that your enemy is going to strike you, it is usually not wise to wait until he gets the jump on you by taking the initiative," Stimson testified after the war. "In spite of the risk involved, however, in letting the Japanese fire the first shot, we realized that in order to have the full support of the American people it was desirable to make sure that the Japanese be the ones to do this so that there would remain no doubt in anyone's mind as to who were the aggressors."[57]

In May 1946 the victorious powers that had defeated Japan convened a tribunal in Tokyo that indicted and tried twenty-eight Japanese military and political leaders with "crimes against peace" (another 5,700 Japanese nationals were charged with traditional war crimes and "crimes against humanity"). The International Military Tribunal for the Far East (IMTFE), also known as the Tokyo War Crimes Trials, adjourned in November 1948 after sentencing seven defendants—including Hideki Tojo—to death, sixteen to life imprisonment, and two to lesser prison terms. (Charges were dropped against three defendants.) In its final judgment the tribunal noted "the contention advanced on behalf of the defendants that Japan's acts of aggression against France, her attack on the Netherlands, and her attacks on Great Britain and the United States of America were justifiable measures of self-defense. It is argued that these Powers took such measures to restrict the economy of Japan that she had no way of preserving the welfare and prosperity of her nationals but to go to war." The IMTFE emphatically rejected the defendants' argument, contending instead that Western economic sanctions against Japan were "an entirely justifiable attempt to induce Japan to depart from the course of aggression on which she had long embarked and upon which she had determined to continue." The tribunal pointed out that the United States gave notice of its intent to terminate its Treaty of Commerce and Navigation with Japan only after Japan had seized Manchuria and much of the rest of China. Thereafter, "the successive embargoes which were imposed on the export of materials to Japan were imposed as it became clearer and clearer that Japan had determined to attack the territories and interests of the Powers." Sanctions were imposed "to induce Japan to depart from her aggressive policy . . . and in order that the Powers might no longer supply Japan with the materials to wage war upon them." Given this judgment, the tribunal predictably concluded that the attacks that Japan launched on December 7, 1941, against the United States, Great Britain, and the Netherlands "were unprovoked attacks, prompted by the desire to seize the possessions of these nations" and that "[w]hatever may be the difficulty of stating a comprehensive definition of 'a war of aggression', attacks made with the above motive cannot but be characterized as wars of aggression."[58]

CHAPTER FOUR

Japanese Assumptions and Decision Making

During the 1930s and early 1940s Japanese foreign policy was dedicated to the establishment by force of an empire encompassing all of East Asia. The Japanese viewed international relations in Social Darwinian terms—i.e., as a pitiless struggle for power in which only the fittest survived. The drive for empire was motivated not by transcendent ideals or universal principles but rather by cold calculation and opportunism. From the time of the Meiji Restoration the Japanese had sought security and status through empire. Having barely escaped colonization by the West in the latter half of the nineteenth Century, the Japanese, desperate to avoid China's fate, "resolved to beat the Europeans and the Americans at their own game; they would become imperialists along with the best of them." Kenneth Pyle has observed that

> The Meiji Restoration was a profoundly conservative event; it was a nationalist revolution that set out Japan's determination to acquire the power to be the equal of the Western world, or even overtake the Western world. Led by young, low-ranking members of the traditional samurai elite, it was motivated by the values of Japan's long feudal period—values of power, status, realism, and respect for hierarchy. The new Meiji leaders responded to the challenge of the international system not with resistance, but with marked realism, pragmatism, and opportunism. As a result, the Japanese alone among Asian peoples accommodated quickly to the norms, principles, and mores of the imperialist system.[1]

Empire also seemed to be an economic imperative. Japan had a high birth rate and in the 1930s was the most densely populated country in the world; its 73 million people—approximately 5 percent of the world's population—were crammed into but 1 percent of the world's land.[2]

Like Hitler and his entourage in Germany, the Japanese leaders hungered after space for their rapidly growing population. Japan lacked natural resources, and those resources were plentiful in the lands of China and Southeast Asia. Colonization seemed the perfect solution: it would offer an outlet to the surplus population at home, and simultaneously consolidate Japanese power around the western Pacific. Asia was weak and internally divided; it seemed natural to the Japanese that a vigorous and dynamic people like themselves should take over the region and run it properly. Besides, they said, if we don't do it, the Europeans and the Americans will do it for us.[3]

Indeed, the Japanese looked to the Monroe Doctrine and the British Empire as models—and justifications—for their ambitions in East Asia.[4] Had not the United States established itself as the indisputable hegemon in its own region in the world—and put the world on notice that it would brook no further colonization or recolonization in Latin America by any other great power? And had not the British, a small island people like the Japanese, constructed a global empire based on a measure of naval domination that Japan had worked so hard to obtain in the Western Pacific? And was not Great Britain's standing as a great power wholly a function of its possession of a vast empire?

Race was no less a factor in the drive for empire. The Japanese believed they were racially destined to dominate Asia because they regarded themselves as the divine Yamato race—superior to all other Asian (and European) races. "It was the intention of the Japanese to establish permanent domination over all other races and peoples in Asia—in accordance with their needs, and as befitted their destiny as a superior race," observes John Dower. Like the Nazis, the Japanese viewed the world as a racial hierarchy in which each people should be treated in accordance with their racial characteristics and abilities. The Japanese vision of empire was one of permanent inequality of racial rank.

[T]he Japanese plan for the [Greater East Asian] Co-Prosperity Sphere amounted to an almost perfect model of "center-periphery" relationships, all designed to ensure the supremacy of the Japanese as the leading race. In this scheme, Japan was the towering metropole, the overwhelmingly dominant hub of the great autarkic bloc. All currency and finance would naturally be tied to the yen. All major transportation and communications networks . . . were to center on Japan and be controlled by Tokyo. All war-related industrial production, energy resources, and strategic materials would likewise be controlled by Tokyo. Japan would be responsible for the production of high-quality manufactures and finished products in the heavy-industry sector. While Japan would provide capital and technical know-how for the development of light industry (generally for local consumption) throughout the Co-Prosperity Sphere, most countries would remain in their familiar roles as producers of raw materials and semi-finished goods. [5]

Japanese domination of East Asia required the expulsion of Western power and influence from both China and Southeast Asia. Yet it was most unlikely that the United States, Great Britain, France, and the Netherlands would depart without a fight. All had colonies in the Far East, regarded Southeast Asian sea lines of communication as strategically vital, and rejected Japan's claim of a "right" to empire in East Asia at the expense a Western colonial presence in Southeast Asia. Japan's drive for empire thus meant probable war with one or more of the Western powers, including the United States, the dominant naval power in the Eastern Pacific and the leading proponent of the very liberal international political and economic order Japanese militarists so despised.

The Japanese brought a number of beliefs, or assumptions, to their consideration of war with the United States. Some were realistic, others not, and the line between reasonable expectation and wishful thinking was often blurred. The first assumption was that Germany would continue to tie down British and Soviet military power in Europe and the Mediterranean. Though by December of 1941 Britain remained in the war and the Soviet Union appeared to have survived the German onslaught (at least until the spring of 1942), neither was in a position to affect the outcome of a war in the Pacific. Moreover, the German threat in Europe and the North Atlantic would continue to command America's primary strategic attention. From the fall of France in the summer of 1940 through the German invasion of Russia the following summer, the Roosevelt administration made it plain, through both word and deed, that it regarded events in Europe as more threatening—and therefore more important—to the United States than events in Far East. The Japanese clearly understood that prospects for expanding their empire into Southeast Asia and sustaining it depended on the success of German arms in Europe, and many Japanese believed, at least before the battles of Stalingrad and El Alamein, that the Germans would win the war. "The big hope was that the Americans, confronted by a German victory in Europe and weary of the war in the Pacific, would agree to a negotiated peace in which Japan would be recognized as the dominant power in Eastern Asia," observed Nobutaka Ike in his indispensable 1967 translation and edit, *Japan's Decision for War: Records of the 1941 Policy Conferences*.[6]

The second assumption was that the United States and Great Britain were strategically indivisible—more specifically, that a Japanese attack on British possessions in Southeast Asia would mean war with the United States. If Americans viewed Germany, Japan, and Italy as a cohesive bloc of aggressor states, the Japanese viewed the United States and Britain, which in 1941 were cooperating mightily against Germany in Europe, as strategically inseparable in the Far East. On this issue opinion was at first divided between the army and the navy. "The fundamental difference between the two services arose over the military consequences of any advance to the south," contends Michael Barnhart. "The army initially hoped that military operations, if they proved necessary, could be confined to Dutch or, at worst, Anglo-Dutch targets. The United States was not to be involved, the Philippines not to be attacked."[7] The IJA's position suggested a view that the United States and

Britain might be separated over the defense of British possessions in Southeast Asia if the Japanese left the Americans alone.[8] But the IJA's position ran afoul of the IJN's view that the United States and Britain were strategically inseparable, and therefore that an attack on non-U.S. targets in Southeast Asia would invite an American counterattack on the exposed left flank of southward-advancing Japanese forces. According to Robert Butow, the IJN "adamantly asserted that it was absolutely impossible to think of Britain and the United States as separate entities; consequently, an attack upon the Philippines would be a prerequisite for a successful advance to the South."[9] The army's stance also ignored the IJN's bureaucratic and strategic requirements. Because Anglo-Dutch naval forces in the region were weak, "the navy saw no role for itself in any advance limited to those countries' possessions. The fleet then would not be positioned to demand the materials allocations necessary for the completion of current building plans, much less the initiation of new ones."[10]

The IJN's views were incorporated in a navy-drafted assessment provided to the government on October 28, 1941. In a prepared written response to the question of whether or not Japan's enemies in Southeast Asia could be strategically separated, the navy asserted that "Undoubtedly, an understanding exists between Great Britain, the United States and the Netherlands to stand united in the event of an armed invasion of the southern area by Japan." (In fact, though senior-level Anglo-American military staff talks had begun in Washington in January 1941, Roosevelt refused to commit the United States to a defense of British or Dutch territory in Southeast Asia.) While conceding that the timing and nature of armed responses by the three might differ, the assessment emphatically concluded that "limitation of the adversary to the Netherlands, or to Great Britain and the Netherlands, would be absolutely impossible." Though the United States "might not actively enter the war immediately," resorting instead "to feints in order to gain time to reinforce her military strength," she would nonetheless "enter a war against Japan as soon as possible" because the United States "considers that she has a voice in the southwest Pacific area" and "needs such raw materials as rubber and tin from this area." Additionally, "Military action by Japan would menace the Philippines," and the United States "would completely lose her voice in Chinese affairs if she did not enter the Pacific war." Finally, "United States public opinion would be much more likely to favor defense of the Pacific than of Europe."[11]

The IJN's view ultimately prevailed, and in so doing left unanswered the intriguing historical question of what the United States could or would have done in response to a Japanese invasion of Southeast Asia confined only to Europe's colonial possessions. Barnhart believes that Tokyo's refusal "to understand and take advantage of the Roosevelt administration's inability to formally commit the armed forces of the United States to the aid of the British and Dutch unless American territory itself was attacked" was a major Japanese failure.[12] It is not clear that Roosevelt would have asked for a declaration of war; what is clear is that he would have had a difficult time obtaining one from a U.S. Congress (especially the Senate) still heavily populated by isolationists. It is no less clear that the Japanese did not comprehend the domestic political jam they could have put Roosevelt in by bypassing the Philippines and confronting him with the challenge of carrying the country into war on behalf of Europe's colonies in Southeast Asia. In his critique of Japan's strategy, Herbert Rosinski, a naval writer who fled Nazi Germany, observed:

> The Japanese strategists could have carried through that drive [into Southeast Asia] without touching the Philippines merely observing and "masking" them—operating from their advanced concentration areas in the Palau Islands, on Hainan and in Indo-China. From the broader political point of view there would have been in fact every reason for going to the extreme to avoid anything that could contribute to bring the United States into the conflict. But Yamamoto and his collaborators did not see it in that light. To them the intervention of the United States was a foregone conclusion and the only "realistic" policy to nip that intervention in the bud [was] by temporarily crippling her by a surprise attack against her naval forces and bases in the Pacific. For that reason the violent conflict between those Japanese Admirals who wanted to concentrate *all*

forces upon the drive to the south and those who contended that it would need to be "secured" by an attack upon the Pacific Fleet at Pearl Harbor, was finally decided in favor of the latter by Admiral Nagano.[13]

The third Japanese assumption was that time was working against Japan—i.e., the longer Japan waited to initiate war against the United States, the dimmer its prospects for success. This assumption was grimly realistic. As the embargo took hold and the United States accelerated its rearmament, Japan's economic and military power vis-à-vis that of the United States began to decline rapidly. Japan had placed its economy on a total-war footing in 1936, whereas the United States was just getting started. In the critical category of naval tonnage, Japan in late 1941 possessed a competitive 70 percent of total U.S. naval tonnage (including tonnage deployed in the Atlantic), but the Japanese correctly projected, based on existing naval building programs (and excluding estimated losses), that the ratio would drop to 65 percent in 1942, 50 percent in 1943, and 30 percent in 1944.[14] The Two-Ocean Navy Act passed by Congress in July 1940 called for a 70 percent increase in U.S. naval tonnage, including construction of 18 aircraft carriers, 6 battleships, 33 cruisers, 115 destroyers, and 43 submarines.[15] H. P. Willmott has observed that the act "doomed the Imperial Navy to second-class status, since the activities of American shipyards would be as catastrophic for Japanese aspirations as a disastrous naval battle would be."[16] Yamamoto had warned Japanese leaders: "Anyone who has seen the auto factories in Detroit and the oil fields in Texas knows that Japan lacks the national power for a naval race with America."[17] Japan's relative naval strength would never be better than in 1941. Indeed, during the war years the United States built 8,812 naval vessels to Japan's 589.[18] A month before Pearl Harbor, Army Chief of Staff Hajime Sugiyama warned that "the ratio of armament between Japan and the United States will become more unfavorable to us as time passes; and particularly, the gap in air armament will enlarge rapidly."[19] In 1941 the United States produced 1,400 combat aircraft to Japan's 3,200; three years later, the United States built 37,500 to Japan's 8,300.[20]

Thus the oil embargo drove the Japanese into the logic of preventive war: given war's inevitability and Japan's declining military power relative to the enemy's, Japanese leaders reasoned, better war now than later. However poor Japan's chances of defeating the United States, they were better in 1941 than in any coming year. At the time of the Pearl Harbor attack, the Pacific Ocean warship balance between Japan and the United States was 10:8 in battleships, 10:3 in aircraft carriers, 18:13 in heavy cruisers, 20:11 in light cruisers, 112:80 in destroyers, and 65:56 in submarines.[21]

A fourth and equally realistic assumption was that Japan had little chance of winning a protracted war with the United States. America's great material superiority would eventually bury Japan. If Japan had any chance of fighting a war with the United States to some kind of successful conclusion, it had to bring military operations to a head as soon as possible. As Yamamoto had warned Prime Minister Fumimaro Konoye in the fall of 1940, "if I am told to 'go at it,' you will see me run wild for half a year, maybe a year. But I have no confidence whatsoever when it comes to two years, three years."[22] Admiral Osami Nagano, the IJN's chief of staff, clearly understood that a protracted war benefited the United States. Indeed, he believed that "the probability is very high that they [the United States] will from the outset plan on a prolonged war. Therefore it will be necessary for us to be reconciled to this and to be prepared militarily for a long war." He hoped that the United States would "aim for a quick war leading to an early decision, send[ing] their principal naval units [into the Western Pacific], and challeng[ing] us to an immediate war," but he feared that "America will attempt to prolong the war, using her impregnable position, her superior industrial power, and her abundant resources."[23] Neither Nagano nor any other Japanese leader offered a practical alternative to fighting a war on U.S. terms. Small, short-war Japan was going to pick a fight with huge, long-war America.

Given the expectation of a long war with the United States, how did Japan expect to survive, much less win? Did Japanese leaders have a theory of victory, or at least of defeat-avoidance? Japan was not strong enough to threaten the American homeland, but the war was going to be fought in East Asia and the Western Pacific, which the Japanese controlled or would soon control (after Tokyo's conquest of Southeast Asia). Might Tokyo be able to fight the United States to a bloody stalemate on the Japanese side of the Pacific and extract from that stalemate some kind of political settlement with Washington that would preserve Japan's core imperial interests on the Asian mainland?

These questions point to a fifth Japanese assumption, or at least hope: namely, that by swiftly seizing and fortifying the Central and Southwestern Pacific, the Japanese could force the Americans into a murderous, island-by-island slog that would eventually exhaust their political will to fight on to total victory. After the Russo-Japanese War, it had been an article of faith among IJN war planners that a U.S.-Japanese war would entail a Japanese assault on the Philippines, which in turn would provoke a westward dash of the U.S. Fleet across the Pacific, where the IJN, dominant in East Asian waters, would lay in wait. Japan already controlled and was fortifying outposts in the Mariana, Marshall, and Caroline island groups (former German territories mandated by the League of Nations to Japan after World War I). Tokyo would raise the blood and treasure costs of the war beyond Washington's willingness to pay.[24] "The Japanese theory of victory," contends Colin Gray, "amounted to the hope—one hesitates to say calculation—that the United States would judge the cost of defeating Japan to be too heavy, too disproportionate to the worth of the interests at stake."[25]

This strategy was expressed in a document prepared by the Japanese military leadership for the critical Imperial Conference of September 6. The document, "The Essentials for Carrying Out the Empire's Policies," presented a series of questions and answers, one of which was: *What is the outlook in a war with Great Britain and the United States; particularly, how shall we end the war?* The answer:

A war with the United States and Great Britain will be long, and will become a war of endurance. It is very difficult to predict the termination of war, and it would be well-nigh impossible to expect the surrender of the United States. However, we cannot exclude the possibility that the war may end because of a great change

in American public opinion, which may result from such factors
as the remarkable success of our military operations in the South
[Southeast Asia] or the surrender of Great Britain. At any rate, we
should be able to establish an invincible position: by building up
a strategically advantageous position through the occupation of
important areas in the South; by creating an economy that will be
self-sufficient in the long run through the development of rich resources in the Southern regions, as well as through the use of the
economic power of the East Asian continent; and by linking Asia
and Europe in destroying the Anglo-American coalition through
our cooperation with Germany and Italy. Meanwhile, we may hope
that we will be able to influence the trend of affairs and bring the
war to an end. [26]

Nagano, who initially opposed war with the United States but subsequently became a strong advocate of immediate action because of
Japan's accelerating military decline relative to the United States, believed that

If we take the South, we will be able to strike a strong blow against
American resources of national defense. That is, we will build an
iron wall, and within it we will destroy, one by one, the enemy
states in Asia; and in addition, we will defeat America and Britain. If Britain is defeated, Americans will have to do some thinking.
When we are asked what will happen in five years from now, it is
natural that we should not know, whether it is in military operations, politics, or diplomacy.[27]

Nagano believed Japan could convert the Southwestern Pacific into
an "impregnable" bastion, "laying the basis for protracted operations"
that would exhaust U.S. will.[28] Adrian Lewis believes this best explains
the Japanese determination to wage a "hopeless" resistance in the Central Pacific from 1943 to 1945:

While the Marines fought some very difficult and bloody battles
in places such as Tarawa and Iwo Jima, there was, in fact, *no way*

for them to lose. The Japanese had no way to reinforce, no way to resupply, no way to evacuate, no way to equal the firepower of the U.S. Navy, and frequently no air power. The Japanese literally had no way to win or survive. . . . The Japanese recognized their fate. They well understood the futility of their situation. However, their objective was not to achieve victory in the traditional sense. Their objective was to inflict as many casualties as possible on American forces, to hold out as long as possible, and to prolong the war. The Japanese believed they could destroy the will of the American people.[29]

Michael Bess has lucidly summarized the reasoning behind Japan's "iron wall" strategy, which, the Japanese hoped, would confront the United States with a painful choice:

[The Americans] can come and fight us to liberate those territories, or they can accept the fact that the map of Asia has been redrawn, and that they must henceforth learn to deal with a Japanese-led Asian bloc. If we make it clear that kicking us Japanese out of our new Asian empire is going to require a long, bloody fight, then there is a good chance that the Americans will regard the battle as simply not being worth the cost in lives. Controlling the southwestern Pacific is not a vital interest of the United States. The American people will say: Why should the United States fight a protracted war, merely to give back to the British and Dutch and French their Asian colonies? Why should we send our citizens to fight and die, merely to regain possession of a worthless protectorate in the Philippines? Antiwar movements will spread, and in the end, the American government will simply have to accept Japan's fait accompli. They may not like it, but they won't have the popular support to do much about it. Japan's best ally . . . will be the deepseated American tendency toward isolationism. As long as no vital American interests are in play, the Yankees can be counted on to stay put.[30]

The Japanese, as it turned out, were correct in assuming that they could impose a protracted war of attrition on the Americans. They employed a combination of distance and fanatical resistance to force the Americans to grind their way, island by island, bloody assault by bloody assault, across the vast expanses of the Central and Southwestern Pacific. Yet a war of attrition with the United States was a war Japan was destined to lose—unless America's overwhelming capacity for war was subverted by lack of political will to pay the necessary price. The Japanese, however, had eliminated that possibility by their surprise attack on Pearl Harbor. How hard would the Americans have fought if the Japanese had not attacked the Philippines and Hawaii on December 7, 1941? Would they have fought at all?

Underlying the Japanese belief that they could bleed the Americans into a political settlement short of total victory—a belief that persisted among the Japanese military leadership well into 1945—was a sixth assumption: Japanese racial and spiritual superiority could neutralize America's material superiority. Japan was neither the first nor the last of America's enemies to stress the superiority of the human element of war and to underestimate the resolve of Americans at war. The Japanese were fully aware of their industrial weakness vis-à-vis the United States; they had long believed, however, that the unique qualities of their race, including a superior national will, discipline, and war-fighting prowess, could defeat the strong but soft Americans. "The Japanese regarded us as a decadent nation in which pacifism and isolationism practically ruled the policy of our government," testified Ambassador Grew after the war.[31] In December 1939 Grew had warned that attempts to defeat Japan via economic sanctions ignored Japanese psychology. "Japan is a nation of hardy warriors, still inculcated with the samurai do-or-die spirit which has by tradition and inheritance become ingrained in the race." Grew went on to note that the "Japanese throughout their history have faced periodic cataclysms brought about by nature and by man: earthquakes, hurricanes, floods, epidemics, the blighting of crops, and almost constant wars within and without the country. By long experience they are inured to hardship . . . and to regimentation."[32]

H. P. Willmott points out that modern Japan was, in 1941, "a nation with no experience of defeat and, more importantly, a nation [that believed itself] created by gods, and ruled by a god. . . . This religious dimension provided the basis for the belief in the superiority of the Japanese martial commitment . . . that was the guarantee against national defeat."[33] As for America, many Japanese shared the view of Rear Admiral Tasuku Nakazawa, chief of the IJA's operations section: "a composite nation of immigrants [which] lacked unity, could not withstand adversity and privations, and regarded war as a form of sport, so that if we deal a severe blow at the outset of hostilities they would lose the will to fight."[34] As John Dower observes, in Japanese eyes

> all Westerners were assumed to be selfish and egoistic, and incapable of mobilizing for a long fight in a distant place. All the "Western" values which Japanese ideologues and militarists had been condemning since the 1930s, after all, were attacked because they were said to sap the nation's strength and collective will. More concretely, it was assumed that Great Britain would fall to the Germans, and the United States war effort would be undercut by any number of debilitating forces endemic to contemporary America's isolationist sentiment, labor agitation, racial strife, political factionalism, capitalistic or "plutocratic" profiteering, and so on.[35]

As a creature-comforted capitalist society, America was simply too soft to sustain the blood and treasure burdens of a long, harsh war, especially in a region where the strength of U.S. interests was weak relative to the strength of Japanese interests, and at some point the capitalists who controlled the United States would turn against a war whose balance sheet was registering far more costs than benefits. "The [Japanese] military went into the Pacific War still clinging to the concept of fighting spirit as decisive in battle," notes Saburo Ienaga. "The result was wanton waste of Japanese lives, particularly in combat with Allied forces whose doctrine was based on scientific rationality."[36]

Indeed, as John A. Lynn has pointed out, absent Japanese racial stereotyping of Americans as "soft, self-indulgent, and incapable of

serious sacrifice . . . Japanese war plans did not make sense, since Tokyo realized that the advantages of numbers in manpower and mate-
riel always rested with the United States."[37] Japan's industrial poverty
relative to that of the Soviet Union and the United States virtually dictated an embrace of spiritual power over material strength. Even after
its punishing defeat at Nomohan, which should have alerted the IJA to
the perils of warring with an industrial giant like the United States, the
IJA's operational thinking remained essentially primitive, unscientific,
complacent, narrow, and simplistic. Reaffirmation of faith in moral at-
tributes and psychological factors amounted to callous evasion of the realities of modern firepower, mechanization, and aviation. The rationale
was that the quantity and quality of the material possessed by Japan's
enemies—and their sheer numbers—could only be offset by intangible
factors such as high morale, spirit, and fearlessness in close fighting
against men and armor. At Nomohan and throughout the Pacific War,
the price was paid in lives squandered in desperate banzai charges with
the bayonet, though it was well known that frontal assaults had rarely
succeeded since the days of the Russo-Japanese War.[38]

Japanese illusions about "American decadence and effeteness and
their failure to appreciate [America's] self-confidence and absolutist
view of war rooted in the liberal tradition," observes Richard Betts,
"facilitated the miscalculation that Washington would make the cost-
benefit calculations Tokyo hoped [for]: accept limited war and sue for
peace after severe initial setbacks and the establishment of a Japanese
perimeter in the Pacific that would be costly to crack."[39]

Scott Sagan, in his assessment of the Japanese decision for war
against the United States, argues that the "persistent theme of Japanese
irrationality is highly misleading, for, using the common standard in
the literature (a conscious calculation to maximize utility based on a
consistent value system), the Japanese decision for war appears to have
been rational." Sagan goes on to assert that upon close examination of
the decisions made in Tokyo in 1941, "one finds not a thoughtless rush

to national suicide, but rather a prolonged, agonizing debate between two repugnant alternatives."[40]

The decisions were made by a small group of senior civilian officials and IJA and IJN officers, all of whom were committed to Japan's continued imperial expansion, regarded the United States as the main obstacle to that expansion, and opposed making any significant concessions to the United States. There were differences of opinion on timing and sequencing, and on the utility of negotiations, and the emperor, Prince Konoye (three times prime minister from 1937 to 1941), and senior naval officers were markedly more reluctant to risk war with the United States than the army's leadership. But no senior Japanese military or political figure was prepared to renounce empire or submit to American dictation. As Langer and Gleason observed of the Japanese leadership as it entered the late summer of 1941:

> The Japanese might be divided on the question of what direction and method to choose for expansion and conquest, but there is no evidence that any important figure, civilian or military, was prepared to abandon aspirations which were truly national. Prince Konoye was distinguished from his colleagues only insofar as he posed as a man of good will and hoped, probably sincerely, that he could attain by negotiation what the military men recognized could be won only by force of arms. By and large, Japanese leaders seem to have believed, along with statesmen throughout the world, that Hitler's victory over Soviet Russia was imminent and that thereafter the Axis would be so powerful that the United States would be obliged to concentrate all its attention and power on the Atlantic.[41]

A universal commitment to imperial expansion, however, did not mean a capacity for strategic coherence. Unlike the United States and Great Britain, Japan lacked a civil authority able and willing to impose a coherent strategy on an army and navy that had contradictory operational outlooks and agendas and that regarded one another with almost as much suspicion as any foreign enemy. Japan had no equivalent of a Roosevelt or Churchill—i.e., a strong and competent civil authority constitutionally empowered to formulate a grand strategy and to subordinate the instruments of force to that strategy. The emperor was titular and passive. Though he "theoretically retained, and in an emergency could occasionally wield, absolute powers, and though he maintained an intelligent interest in government affairs, his office was so hedged about with advisers and the performance of so many routine functions that his influence on policy was limited."[42] A foreign ministry official described the emperor's position as merely "the reflection of the moon in the water and not the moon shining in the sky." He was "at once a godlike symbol and an empty figurehead. The real moon was the military who exercised the power and enjoyed all its benefits. God and Caesar were synthesized in the crown, but the Emperor was actually neither the one nor the other."[43] The fact that both the emperor and Prince Konoye, prime minister from 1937 to 1939 and from July 1940 to October 1941, strongly opposed war with the United States speaks volumes about the absence of effective civilian control over the Japanese military. Indeed, Donald M. Goldstein and Katherine V. Dillon believe that

> for most if not all of 1941 Japanese-U.S. diplomacy was irrelevant. Japan's extremists, saber-rattling elements were in the saddle. It was a cliché of the time that the Emperor of Japan was a puppet; there was less realization that the Prime Minister and Foreign Minister were almost equally so. The military had a stranglehold on the Japanese government so that any agreement reached between the Foreign Ministry and the State Department would be meaningless unless the Japanese military supported it. And the Japanese military—particularly the Army—was not interested in peace; it was interested in conquest and power.[44]

Militarists—military officers and civilians who believed in a militarized society and foreign policy—ran the country and its foreign policy, and what passed for strategy was little more than the product of bargaining between the army and navy, which cooperated only when they had to. The army, the politically dominant service, looked east, to the Asian mainland, and north, to its old enemy, Russia; it was preoccupied with subduing China and eventually conquering the Soviet Far East. The army welcomed the Tripartite Pact and the German invasion of Russia in June 1941. The navy looked south, to the weakly defended oil-rich Dutch East Indies and rubber- and tin-rich British Malaya; it opposed Japan's alliance with Germany. Moreover, the navy had "a wholesome respect for the prowess of the British and the American navies, and along with the civilian leaders a clearer perception of Japan's weaknesses and of the strength that would oppose them than did the Army with its more parochial attitude."[45] Key senior naval officers, including Yamamoto, opposed the Tripartite Pact, at least insofar as it could be interpreted as mandating war with the United States in the event of a German-American war.

Because the army and navy "could not define a common opponent, they independently calculated their force structure based on differing hypothetical enemies," observes Edward Drea. "The number of divisions needed to win a war against Russia became the army's yardstick whereas the U.S. Navy served as the navy's standard. Neither service would compromise because of the possibility that Japan might have to fight both simultaneously."[46] Indeed, combining the two services' strategic agendas as a national policy portended a naval war with Great Britain and the United States in the Western Pacific, a land war with the Red Army in the Soviet Far East, and a definitive military solution to a war in China that the Japanese could never seem to win. Akira Fujiwara has correctly pointed out that "it was clearly irrational even to consider a policy based on waging war simultaneously against a great land power, Russia, and a great Naval power, the United States," yet such a policy was adopted because "there existed no governmental machinery to coordinate and establish priorities between the demands of the two services."[47]

The postwar United States Strategic Bombing Survey described the Japanese government as an "oligarchy, a coalition of factions of the ruling class," which included the army, navy, zaibatsu (Japanese business conglomerates), aristocrats and elder statesmen. According to the survey:

political policy was set through a curious process of bargaining, which involved an almost perpetual forming and reforming of coalitions within the oligarchy. The process required a careful consultation of all factions and unanimity among leaders before the government could take a major policy step. These [five] groups, through the political institutions they controlled, assumed collective responsibility for the actions of government. Such responsibility, of course, was taken in the name of the Emperor, though it was the result of manipulation among the factions.[48]

Civilian leaders, such as Konoye, were thoroughly committed to the military's imperial agenda, though they sometimes differed with military leaders over timing and sequencing. Yale Candee Maxon contends that "it was the willingness of Konoye and other civilian puppets to front for the Army which enabled the latter to pursue its irresponsible course while civilian officials of the government shouldered formal responsibility."[49]

The army was in fact the main force behind Japan's reckless imperial expansion during the decade separating the seizure of Manchuria and the attack on Pearl Harbor. It was not only a politically dominant and pro-Nazi alliance but also the source of assassinations and attempted assassinations of civilian and military officials who opposed army policy. According to one assessment of Japanese foreign policy:

> During the decade and more preceding Pearl Harbor a conflict went on within the Japanese Government between a dominant group within the Army, which insisted upon plunging the country into a course of forcible expansion, and civilian and Navy leaders, who were either opposed to such a course or perceived grave risks in it. Each successive step toward the fulfillment of expansionist aims was taken on the initiative of the Army, often in defiance of constituted authority, until finally the moderates lost control of the situation altogether and an Army-dictated Cabinet under Prince Konoye came into office in July 1940.[50]

Hull testified after the war that

We knew that Japanese leaders were unreliable and treacherous. We asked ourselves whether the military element in Japan would permit the civilian element, even if so disposed, to stop Japan's course of expansion by force and to revert to peaceful courses. Time and again the civilian leaders gave assurances; time and again the military took aggressive action in direct violation of those assurances. Japan's past and contemporary record was replete with instances of military aggression and expansion by force. Since 1931 and especially since 1937 the military in Japan exercised a controlling voice in Japan's national policy.[51]

The main decision-making venue was the Liaison Conferences, of which fifty-six leading to the decision for war were held from April 18 through December 4, 1941.[52] The conferences brought together representatives of the Cabinet—the prime minister, the foreign minister, the war minister, the navy minister, and sometimes other ministers of state—and the army and navy chiefs of staff and vice chiefs of staff. Major policy decisions reached at Liaison Conferences were forwarded to Imperial Conferences for pro forma approval by the emperor. Indeed, it was "very unusual to convene an Imperial Conference without arranging beforehand both the agenda and the final decision." Debates were "usually perfunctory, and . . . the conferences were held merely to maintain the fiction that the Emperor sanctioned the decisions in person."[53] Attendees at an imperial conference, which met in the presence of the emperor, who almost always remained silent, included members of the Liaison Conference along with the president of the Privy Council, who served as the emperor's spokesman.[54] It is testimony to the emperor's limited influence that while he was personally against hostilities with the United States and managed to delay the decision for war for six weeks, he "eventually succumbed to the persistent pressure of the military bureaucracy and accepted its argument that war with the United States was inevitable and possibly winnable."[55]

Military opinion necessarily dominated Liaison Conference discussions and decisions, given that at least six of the eight principals were serving officers (in May 1936 the government revived an old rule that the navy and war ministers had to be on the active list with the rank of lieutenant general or above); war minister Hideki Tojo made it seven when he became prime minister in October 1941, a position he held until 1944. (Of the eleven prime ministers who served Japan from May 1932 to August 1945, four were admirals and four were generals; only three were civilians.[56]) Indeed, conference deliberations "were utilized principally to sanction foreign policies which originated within the military."[57] The Liaison Conferences also reveal a refusal to confront openly the possibility of defeat and its probable consequences, and a pervasive fatalistic belief that Japan's destiny was in the hands of forces beyond the control of Japanese decision makers.[58] There were also sharp divisions between IJA and IJN representatives over timing and methods, but they all shared the same basic values, including a belief in death before dishonor.

The IJN leadership had a much greater knowledge of the United States and respect for its power than did the IJA leadership. Nagano, Yamamoto, and other senior naval officers had spent considerable time in the United States as attachés and participants in various conferences; in fact, half of all IJN officers with the rank of captain or above had served abroad, most of them in Britain or the United States.[59] The IJN's leadership did not want war with the United States but ultimately reversed its position because, as Sadao Asada has pointed out, it could not "dare openly admit" that it "was not capable of fighting the United States" because "such a confession of weakness would seriously jeopardize the morale of naval officers and call into question the raison d'etre of the imperial navy itself." Against the United States, the IJN "was an instrument of deterrence, not of war."[60] One can only speculate on the consequences for Japan and the United States had the IJN's leadership mustered the moral courage to declare emphatically to the army and the emperor that it could not hope to defeat the U.S. Navy, at least in a war that the Americans were in a position to prolong until they amassed overwhelming power.

In contrast, Tojo and other senior IJA officers were fixated upon the war in China and had long regarded Russia as Japan's principal enemy. The IJA had no plans or strategy for a war against the United States and never made any real attempt to evaluate the United States as an enemy.[61] Indeed, the IJA leadership believed that war with the United States was the navy's responsibility. "So long as the navy failed to declare unequivocally that there was no chance of victory [against the United States], the army saw no reason to concern itself with the problem."[62] This extraordinarily casual attitude toward the United States, an enemy for which the IJA had performed no military assessment or drafted a war plan, was the product in part of the army's utter preoccupation with its responsibilities on the Asian mainland. At the time of the Pearl Harbor attack, the army had a million troops in China, 700,000 troops in Manchuria (for a possible invasion of Siberia) and had already sustained 180,000 dead and 425,000 wounded in the China war; only eleven of its fifty-one divisions were available for operations in Southeast Asia.[63]

The army marched off to war against the West with no means to defeat the United States, much less an allied coalition. It never reconciled its traditional dilemma over a short-term or a protracted war, and its over-reliance on Nazi Germany to defeat Britain only made an already flawed strategy even weaker. There was no strategic or operational plan after the first six months of hostilities and no thoughtful consideration given to war termination. Trusting in the military prowess of Nazi Germany, army leaders counted on Japan's intangible qualities to overcome a decadent United States.[64]

Only in September 1943 did the IJA's inspector-general of military education direct that army schools switch the focus of their curricula away from war with the Soviet Union toward war with the United States, and not until the summer of 1944 did Imperial General Headquarters issue a tactical manual on island defense against amphibious assault.[65]

Perhaps the most important conference of the year was the Imperial Conference of July 2, 1941. It was at this conference that the emperor sanctioned army and navy plans to acquire bases in southern French Indochina, a move that explicitly postponed consideration of war with the

Soviet Union (until the spring of 1942, assuming Russia's defeat west of the Urals) and greatly increased the risk of war with the United States.[66] The German invasion of Russia on June 22 had persuaded Foreign Minister Yosuke Matsuoka and Privy Council President Yoshimichi Hara, among others, that Japan should strike northward, into the Soviet Far East, before moving southward into Southeast Asia. The "war between Germany and the Soviet Union represents the chance of a lifetime for Japan," argued Hara. "Since the Soviet Union is promoting Communism around the world, we will have to attack her sooner or later. . . . Our Empire wants to avoid going to war with Great Britain and the United States while we are engaged in a war with the Soviet Union. . . . [so] I want to see the Soviet Union attacked on this occasion."[67] However, proponents of a southward advance first prevailed, leaving an attack on Russia for later consideration. U.S. economic sanctions were beginning to bite hard, and there was nothing to stop the Americans from imposing additional sanctions, including an oil embargo. Moreover, Japanese military intelligence was not persuaded that Germany would swiftly defeat the Soviet Union in 1941.[68] The conquest of Southeast Asia would afford Japan control over the oil of the Dutch East Indies as well as the tin and rubber of Malaya and southern Indochina; it would also isolate the Nationalist Government in China from any further Western assistance. The Siberian option could wait.

The policy document approved at the Imperial Conference of July 2, titled "Outline of National Policies in View of the Changing Situation," was quite clear on the implications for Japanese-American relations: "In order to achieve the objectives [of defeating China and securing control of Southeast Asia], preparations for war with Great Britain and the United States will be made. . . . *[O]ur Empire will not be deterred by the possibility of being involved in a war with Great Britain and the United States.*"[69] Thus the momentous decision to go south—to occupy southern Indochina as a preparatory step to a military advance into Southeast Asia—was taken *before* the Roosevelt administration's imposition of an oil embargo. As we have seen, the embargo was a *response* to that decision; indeed, Roosevelt knew of the decision by July 8 through decrypted intercepts of encoded Japanese Foreign Ministry transmissions from Tokyo to Berlin.[70] The Japanese decision to go south was made against the backdrop of escalating U.S. economic warfare against Tokyo and the prescient Japanese fear that harsher sanctions were in the offing, though the abruptness and scope of the asset freeze came as a shock. For Japanese leaders, many of them now persuaded that war with the United States was inevitable, the decision was an economic insurance policy against a complete shutdown of Western trade triggered by the freezing of Japanese assets in the United States on July 26.

At the Imperial Conference on September 6, both IJN Chief of Staff Nagano and IJA Chief of Staff Hajime Sugiyama conceded that a war with the United States would likely be prolonged, but they also contended that the U.S. embargo had made war necessary, and the sooner the better because Japan's national defense capability was declining vis-à-vis that of the United States.[71] In a series of questions and answers prepared for the emperor by the War and Navy ministries, entitled "The Essentials for Carrying Out the Empire's Policies," the proponents of war declared that "the policies of Japan and the United States are mutually incompatible; it is historically inevitable that the conflict between the two countries . . . will ultimately lead to war." The document went on the assert that "Even if we should make concessions to the United States by giving up part of our national policy for the sake of temporary peace, the United States, its military position strengthened, is sure to demand more and more concessions on our part; and ultimately our empire will have to lie prostrate at the feet of the United States."[72] The objective of war was clear:

> to expel the influence of [the United States, Great Britain, and the Netherlands] from East Asia, to establish a sphere for the self-defense and self-preservation of our Empire, and to build a New Order in Greater East Asia. In other words, we aim to establish a close and inseparable relationship in military, political, and economic affairs between our Empire and the countries of the Southern Region, to achieve our Empire's self-defense and self-preservation.[73]

The September 6 Imperial Conference was also noteworthy because the emperor, who rarely spoke, expressed concern that "The Essentials for Carrying Out the Empire's Policies" focused mainly on war rather than possible diplomatic solutions to deteriorating U.S.-Japanese relations. Emperor Hirohito, like Prime Minister Fumimaro Konoye, greatly feared war with the United States, especially against the backdrop of an expanding and seemingly endless war in China. The emperor also doubted Sugiyama's claim that mainland and insular Southeast Asia could be conquered in three months. The following exchange among the emperor, Sugiyama, and Nagano speaks volumes about the Japanese leadership's state of mind in the five months separating the U.S. suspension of exports to Japan and the attack on Pearl Harbor, to say nothing of the strategic dead-end into which the militarists had painted their country.

> *Emperor*: In the event we must finally open hostilities, will our operations have a probability of victory?
>
> *Sugiyama*: Yes, they will.
>
> *Emperor*: At the time of the China Incident [in July 1937], the army told me that we could achieve peace immediately after dealing them one blow with three divisions. Sugiyama, you were my army minister at that time. . . .
>
> *Sugiyama*: China is a continent with a vast hinterland with many ways in and many ways out, and we unexpectedly met big difficulties. . . .
>
> *Emperor* (in great anger): Didn't I caution you each time about those matters? Sugiyama, are you lying to me? If you call the Chinese hinterland vast, would you not describe the Pacific as even more immense? With what confidence do you say "three months"?
>
> *Sugiyama* (stunned, unable to reply)
>
> *Nagano*: If Your Majesty will grant me permission, I would like to make a statement.
>
> *Emperor*: Go ahead.
>
> *Nagano*: There is no 100 percent probability of victory for the troops

stationed there [in China]. . . . Sun Tzu says that in a war between states of similar strength, it is very difficult to calculate
victory. Assume, however, there is a sick person and we leave
him alone; he will definitely die. But if the doctor's diagno-
sis offers a seventy percent chance of survival, provided the
patient is operated on, then don't you think one must try surgery? And if, after the surgery, the patient dies, one must say
that was meant to be. This is indeed the situation we face today. . . . If we waste time, let the days pass, and are forced to
fight after it is too late to fight, then we won't be able to do a
thing about it.

Emperor (in a better mood): All right, I understand. . . . There is no
need to change anything.[74]

Sugiyama was not far off the mark in estimating that it would take
Japanese forces only three months to destroy Western power in Southeast Asia. The British were driven out of Malaya and subsequently surrendered at Singapore on February 15, 1942. Dutch forces in the Netherlands East Indies capitulated on March 8. And the Japanese drove
MacArthur's forces off the Bataan Peninsula on April 19, finally compelling the surrender of the last remaining U.S. resistance in the Philippines, on Corregidor Island, on May 6. Southeast Asia was not China;
Japan's naval power and land-based air power were irresistible and decisive in Southeast Asia in 1941 against the West's weak and scattered
garrisons in the region.

Yet the conquest of Southeast Asia not only eliminated a strategic liability of the United States (the Philippines) but also dissipated Japanese
military power—much of it already mired in China—across a vast new
region that proved difficult to defend against an enemy capable of con-
centrating in ever greater force. Moreover, possession of Southeast Asia,
while providing Japan needed access to heretofore embargoed oil and
other commodity imports, offered no solution to the challenge posed by
expanding—and ultimately overwhelming—U.S. military power. Did
not Sun Tzu's observation imply that predicting the outcome of a war
between states of greatly dissimilar strength was not difficult, or did

Sugiyama really believe that the United States and Japan were more or less evenly matched?

Nagano's postulation of the dying-patient analogy is telling: the Japanese Empire is doomed to die unless the highly risky surgery of an invasion of Southeast Asia (and almost certain war with the United States) is performed. But if the Empire nevertheless dies as a result of the surgery, then "one must say that was meant to be." Such a fatalist interpretation of the Empire's future was pervasive among Japan's militarists, certainly by the late summer of 1941, in part because, one surmises, it absolved them of any responsibility for a decade of cumulatively disastrous decisions that placed Japan in the position where the choice was surrender of empire or war with an enemy Japan could never defeat decisively. In reality the choice was between a surrender compelled by economic sanctions or one compelled by military force—the difference for Japan being, as it turned out, about 2 million military and 350,000 civilian dead and the destruction of Japan's major cities. Nagano's fear about wasting time also underscores the link between Japanese perceptions of the inevitability of war with the United States and the unassailable reality that the military balance was shifting, and for the foreseeable future would continue to shift, decisively against Japan. Only preventive war, it seemed, offered Japan a way out of this dilemma.

The final decisions for war were made at the Liaison Conference of November 1 and the Imperial Conference of November 5. At the Liaison Conference a deadline for military action was set for the beginning of December absent a diplomatic breakthrough by November 30.[75] This deadline was reaffirmed at the Imperial Conference, which also established a set of Japanese negotiating demands which the Roosevelt administration could not possibly accept, thus making war truly inevitable in early December 1941. The demands included non-interference in Japan's war against China; restoration of pre-embargo trade relations; a promise to supply Japan's petroleum needs; and cooperation in obtaining assured Japanese access to the resources of the Dutch East Indies. In exchange, Japan was prepared to foreswear an armed advance into Southeast Asia, except French Indochina.[76] As the Japanese saw it, the

United States was attempting to encircle Japan via assistance to Chiang Kai-shek, strategic collaboration with the British and the Dutch, and the imposition of economic sanctions. "The United States . . . abrogated the Japanese-American Trade Agreement, limited or banned imports and exports, and took other measures to increase her pressure on Japan," declared Foreign Minister Shigenori Togo at the November 5 conference.

Particularly since our Empire concluded the Tripartite Pact, the United States has taken steps to encircle Japan by persuading Great Britain and the Netherlands to join her and by cooperating with the Chiang regime. Since the start of the German-Soviet war, she has taken unfriendly action against us by supplying oil and other war materials to the Soviet Union through the Far East, despite warnings from our Government. As soon as our Empire sent troops into French Indochina after concluding a treaty on the basis of friendly negotiations with the French Government for the purpose of defending ourselves and bringing the China Incident to a conclusion, America's actions became increasingly undisguised. Not only did she cut off economic relations . . . under the guise of freezing our assets, but also, in cooperation with Great Britain, China, and the Netherlands, she threatened the existence of our Empire and tried harder to prevent us from carrying out our national policies. Accordingly, our Empire, which is a stabilizing force in East Asia, was compelled to try to overcome the impasse by showing firmness and determination. [77]

Togo then proceeded to sum up the "present international situation":

In East Asia the British and American policy of aiding Chiang Kai-shek and Japan's encirclement by a coalition of Great Britain, the United States, the Netherlands, and the Chiang regime have been continuously strengthened; and it is possible that the Soviet regime might extend its influence in the Far Eastern area with aid from Great Britain and the United States. Therefore, it cannot be denied that there is a danger that the basis for both the settlement of the

China Incident and the construction of the New Order in East Asia at which our Empire is aiming, might seriously be threatened. In Europe, although Germany and Italy will be able to achieve their first goal, the conquest of the Continent, we cannot anticipate an overall conclusion soon, and the war there is likely to be prolonged. In reality we could not expect Germany and Italy to give us much cooperation. As I see it, the situation is becoming more and more critical every day, and negotiations with the United States are very much restricted by the time element; consequently, to our regret, there is little room for diplomatic maneuvering.[78]

War Minister (and now Prime Minister) Hideki Tojo summarized up the risks and the stakes:

If we enter into a protracted war, there will be difficulties. . . . The first stage of the war will not be difficult. We have some uneasiness about a protracted war. But how can we let the United States to continue to do as she pleases? Two years from now we will have no petroleum for military use. Ships will stop moving. When I think about the strengthening of American defenses in the Southwest Pacific, the expansion of the American fleet, the unfinished China Incident, and so on, I see no end to difficulties. We can talk about austerity and suffering, but can our people endure such a life for a long time? . . . I fear that we would become a third-class nation after two or three years if we just sat tight. . . . America may be enraged for a while, but later she will come to understand [why we did what we did].[79]

Enraged *for a while*? Is it possible that Tojo, who was to guide Japan's destiny for the next three years, believed that a post–Pearl Harbor America's lust for revenge would wear off and that Americans would come to appreciate the necessity for Japan's aggression? If so, it was testimony to a fatal ignorance of America's history and culture.

Planning and training for the attack on Pearl Harbor had begun in early 1941, when Admiral Yamamoto became commander in chief of Japan's Combined Fleet. The final operational plan itself was approved at the September 6 Imperial Conference, and elements of Admiral Chuichi Nagumo's Pearl Harbor strike force began departing Kure naval base on November 10. Ironically, given the strategic consequences of the decision for war with the United States, the attack on Pearl Harbor was much less militarily effective than it could have been. None of the U.S. Pacific Fleet's three aircraft carriers was present at Pearl Harbor on December 7, 1941 (the *Saratoga* was on the West Coast, the *Enterprise* near Wake Island, and the *Lexington* off Midway Island). Of the eight mostly over-aged battleships at Pearl only two (the *Arizona* and *Oklahoma*) were destroyed beyond repair; the rest were refloated, repaired, and returned to wartime service. The same was true of the three light cruisers and four destroyers damaged in the attack. All U.S. heavy cruisers and submarines, and most U.S. destroyers, escaped any damage. Moreover, most of the 155 U.S. combat aircraft destroyed in Hawaii were replaced from the United States mainland within a matter of weeks.[80] Worse still for the Japanese was their failure to destroy Pearl Harbor as a functioning naval base. (The attack was directed against the fleet, not the harbor.) Shore installations, including machine shops and the tremendous oil storage facility adjacent to Pearl Harbor, were left pretty much intact, which permitted the U.S. Navy to continue to operate from Pearl Harbor.

Gordon Prange believed that Nagumo's failure to "pulverize the Pearl Harbor base" and "to seek out and sink America's carriers" was Japan's "first and probably greatest strategic error of the entire Pacific conflict."[81] The destruction of Pearl Harbor or the invasion and occupation of the Hawaiian Islands would have compelled the navy to operate from the American West Coast, adding another three thousand miles of distance to be surmounted before grappling with the Japanese in the Central and Southwestern Pacific. After the war, Minoru Genda, the brilliant Japanese naval aviator who planned the details of the attack on Pearl Harbor, lamented the Japanese failure to invade Hawaii, which he blamed on the IJA's preoccupation with eventual war against the Soviet Union and unwillingness to release (from Manchuria) the divisions necessary to take Hawaii. "After the attack on Pearl Harbor," he said, "we could have taken Honolulu pretty easily. This would have deprived the American Navy of its best island base in the Pacific [and] would have cut the lifeline to Australia, and that country might have fallen to us like a ripe plum."[82] Japanese possession of Hawaii *and* Australia would have deprived the United States of the indispensable base from which to challenge Japanese control of Southeast Asia.

Yet Yamamoto's objective in the Pearl Harbor attack was limited: to knock out the U.S. Pacific Fleet for at least six months so that Japan could conquer Southeast Asia without American naval interference. Pearl Harbor was essentially a flanking raid in support of the main event, which was Tokyo's southward move against Malaya, Singapore, the Philippines, and the Dutch East Indies. Neither Yamamoto nor the IJN's general staff ever seriously considered the possibility of occupying Hawaii, perhaps because the IJA had no divisions to spare for Hawaii. Indeed, but for Yamamoto's insistence to the point of threatened resignation, there would have been no attack on Pearl Harbor. The IJN General Staff opposed the plan because it diverted six aircraft carriers away from the drive into Southeast Asia and because it ran counter to established strategy of luring the U.S. Pacific Fleet into the IJN-dominated Southwestern Pacific. Yamamoto argued that leaving that fleet intact at Pearl Harbor would incur an unacceptable risk by exposing the drive south to a possible U.S. naval assault from the east.[83] Logic seemed to be on Yamamoto's side: if Japan was going to provoke certain war with the United States by attacking the Philippines, why not get in the first blow against the U.S. Pacific Fleet in Hawaii? Moreover, Yamamoto, who understood that carrier-based air power had supplanted battleship-based gun power as the deciding factor in future naval engagements, saw in the U.S. Pacific Fleet's aircraft carriers a threat not only to the IJN's drive south but also to the Japanese home islands themselves. As he queried Admiral Chuichi Nagumo, the IJN's chief of staff, in early October 1941, "But what would you do if, while we were engaged in the South Pacific, the U.S. fleet launched air raids on Japan from the east? Are you suggesting that it's all right for Tokyo and Osaka to be burned to the ground so long as we get hold of oil [in the Dutch East Indies]?"[84]

The absence of the U.S. carriers from Pearl Harbor was truly bad luck for the Japanese. Had the Japanese caught and destroyed or badly damaged the *Saratoga, Enterprise,* and *Lexington* on December 7, 1941, the U.S. Navy probably would not have had sufficient carrier-based air power in the Pacific to thwart, as it did in the Battle of the Coral Sea (May 4–8, 1942), Japan's attempted invasion of Port Moresby, New Guinea, or to challenge, much less decisively defeat, as it did a month later, the Japanese thrust against Midway. There, on June 4–7, U.S. naval forces under Admiral Raymond K. Spruance sank four Japanese carriers.

John Mueller has called the Japanese attack on Pearl Harbor a "military inconvenience" for the United States and a "political and strategic disaster" for Japan because it instantly galvanized American public opinion behind a total war effort that led to Japan's destruction.[85] At one stroke, Pearl Harbor demolished powerful isolationist opposition to Roosevelt's interventionist foreign policy and ensured the eventual defeat of the Axis powers. Conrad Black believes that whatever their tactical success at Pearl Harbor, "the Japanese had committed one of the most catastrophic strategic errors in the history of the nation state, surpassing even the Kaiser's 1917 provocation of the United States."[86] Evans and Peattie believe that by "launching a surprise attack on the U.S. Pacific Fleet, seen by Americans as 'infamous,' the [Japanese] navy created a political, psychological, and, ultimately, strategic climate in the United States that made an unlimited war—a fight to the finish—inevitable." Had the Japanese forgone attacking the Philippines and Hawaii, taking instead only Malaya and the Dutch East Indies, "the war might have had a quite different ending, given the isolationist mood of the United States in late 1941."[87]

Evans and Peattie also contend that even had the Japanese left the U.S. Pacific Fleet alone, "the Americans probably could not have prevented or slowed the lightning progress of Japanese operations in Southeast Asia." The fleet was simply not sufficiently equipped, organized, or battle-experienced to take on Japanese naval and air power in Micronesian waters. Although the United States "could not mount a major trans-Pacific counteroffensive until 1943, this undoubtedly had little to do with the battle damage suffered by the U.S. Navy [at Pearl

Harbor] and much to do with the time and organization necessary to mobilize American industrial might and logistics capabilities for such an undertaking." Evans and Peattie speculate that "Yamamoto would have done better if he had scrapped his Pearl Harbor plan and reverted to the Japanese navy's traditional wait-and-react strategy against a westward-moving American fleet. Certainly such a strategy would have avoided the tidal wave of American public anger at the timing and nature of the actual attack."[88]

Pearl Harbor also testified to the absence of a coherent national strategy. The Japanese leadership was incapable of cutting Japan's imperial ambitions to fit Japan's industrial and military abilities, in large measure because there was no genuine controlling civilian authority to discipline the competing agendas of the IJA and IJN. The politically dominant IJA was especially blind to the limits of Japan's military power and ignorant of the history, culture, and potential fighting power of the United States. Thus, already bogged down in a failed four-year war to subjugate China, the world's most populous country, the Japanese chose to initiate another war, this one against the world's greatest industrial power. And that was not to be the end of it. Once Southeast Asia and the Southwestern Pacific were secured, the Japanese planned to pivot northward. During the summer and fall of 1941 the Japanese planned for war not only against the United States but also against the Soviet Union. In response to Germany's invasion of Russia in June, Japan mobilized army reservists and increased the strength of its Manchuria-based Kwangtung Army from 400,000 to 700,000 men.[89] Tokyo intended to invade Siberia in the spring of 1942 on the assumption that Germany would have defeated or at least sufficiently enfeebled the Soviet Union by then. Akira Iriye has pointed to "the growing tendency among Japanese officials to become fascinated by long-term prospects and to subordinate the goal of settling the war [in China] to visions of future power and glory. The tendency was to damage seriously Japan's ability to cope realistically with existing problems."[90] The imperial overstretch was staggering: to the western front of the gigantic quagmire of the war in China were added two new fronts to the east and south—the Central and Southwestern Pacific, and plans to open a northern front—against the Soviet Union.

Yet even had Japan managed to discipline her imperial ambitions by confining them to Manchuria and insular Southeast Asia, thus freeing up major resources to deal solely with the United States and what remained of British military power in Asia, she would still have been condemned to defeat in a war with America. It was not simply a question of the gaping disparity in industrial might and latent military power between the United States and Japan or of the Japanese army's utter lack of preparedness for war with the United States. The Japanese navy, Tokyo's principal instrument of war against the United States, never really grasped the nature of the Pacific War it initiated at Pearl Harbor. Though Yamamoto and a few other upper-echelon officers not only foresaw the tactical and operational decisiveness of air power but also understood that the war would likely be a protracted, attritional conflict in which the weight of America's industrial and scientific superiority would tell over time, the IJN General Staff, dominated as it was by "battleship" conservatives, remained wedded to the navy's traditional Mahanian belief that the war would be decided by a single, climactic, Tsushima-like battle in which superior gun power would prevail. Though the General Staff grudgingly approved Yamamoto's plan for a surprise attack on Pearl Harbor, the plan was exceptional to the IJN traditional defensive strategy of lying in wait in East Asian waters to ambush a westward advancing U.S. Pacific Fleet. Evans and Peattie convincingly argue that the Japanese navy "neither understood nor prepared for *war* at all. Rather, it believed in and prepared for *battle*." Yet the concept of a single battle that would decide all "no longer had much validity by the twentieth century" because by then "national destinies were measured by the strength or weakness of sinews of national power beyond those purely military: diplomacy, political leadership, trade, economic structure, industrial base, scientific and technological competence, civilian morale, the ability to manipulate public opinion, and the rest of the elements that came to comprise total war."[91] Faith that the IJN could replicate, against the United States, its great victory over Russia in 1905

completely ignored that fact that Russia was utterly incapable of imposing the kind of war on Japan that the United States imposed during the
Pacific War. Even had the Japanese destroyed the entire U.S. Pacific Fleet
in 1941, the loss would have amounted to less than one-half of extant
total U.S. naval tonnage and but a small fraction planned construction.

CHAPTER FIVE

Failed Deterrence

In the fall of 1941, as Nazi armored forces raced toward Moscow, Roosevelt had a lucid sense of where America stood, what it had to do, and the order in which to do it:

> By now—two years into the European war, four years into the Asian war—Roosevelt could see quite clearly where he thought the United States must go. American democracy must engage fascism directly. Germany's hold on the European continent must be broken; Japan's thrust into China and Southeast Asia must be reversed. And he knew the order in which these tasks must be accomplished. Germany must go down first; Japan could wait. In part this ordering reflected Roosevelt's personal familiarity with Europe; having spent, cumulatively, years of his life in Europe, he could visualize Nazi rule far more easily than he could conjure images of the Japanese occupation of China and Indochina. But it also revealed his understanding of the nature of power. Japan, for all its ambitions, remained a comparatively backward, poor country. Conceivably Japan could subdue Chinese resistance, although this seemed less likely now than ever. Possibly it could capture the resources of the East Indies. But not for decades, if ever, would Japan be more than a regional power. Germany, on the other hand, was almost within artillery range of becoming a global power. . . . Roosevelt's reason-

ing caused him to try to provoke a war in the Atlantic even while he attempted to avoid one in the Pacific.[1]

Yet war came in the Pacific notwithstanding Roosevelt's repeated attempts to deter it.

If deterrence is the prevention of action by fear of the consequences, i.e., a state of mind brought about by the existence of a credible threat of unacceptable counteraction, then the United States failed miserably to stop Japan from doing what the United States did not want it to do. It failed to persuade the Japanese that the consequences of contemplated actions were unacceptable. Perhaps the Japanese were simply undeterrable. Perhaps they understood the consequences but were nonetheless driven forward by considerations of honor and unshakeable faith in Japan's divine destiny. Perhaps they preferred suicide to submission.

The Roosevelt administration attempted to deter Japanese expansion into Southeast Asia via three actions: redeployment of most of the U.S. Fleet from southern California to Pearl Harbor in the spring of 1940; imposition of economic sanctions, culminating in the oil embargo of July 1941; and a last-minute attempt to strengthen U.S. military power in Southeast Asia, capped by the deployment to the Philippines of new-production B-17 long-range bombers (and Britain's agreed dispatch of additional warships to the Pacific). The California-based U.S. Fleet, slated to be subdivided into the Atlantic and Pacific Fleets in February 1941, was on maneuvers in Hawaiian waters when Roosevelt ordered it to remain in Pearl Harbor, believing that its open-ended presence there could deter a potential Japanese move into Southeast Asia.[2] When queried by fleet commander Admiral J. O. Richardson as to the purpose of remaining in Hawaiian waters, Admiral Harold "Betty" Stark responded, "You are there because of the deterrent effect which it is thought your presence may have on the Japs going into the East Indies." Stark, who strongly opposed any action that would provoke war with Japan because it would divert U.S. attention and resources away from assisting Great Britain's struggle against Nazi Germany, added that he had no idea of how the United States would react to a Japanese advance into the East Indies. "I don't know and I don't think there is anybody on God's green earth who can tell you."[3]

Unfortunately, the decision to retain the fleet in Hawaii, which was vehemently opposed by Richardson (whom Roosevelt replaced with Admiral Husband Kimmel), exposed the fleet to the very attack the Japanese launched on December 7, 1941. Intended by Roosevelt as a deterrent, the fleet became a magnet. As Yamamoto remarked to a colleague, the "fact that [the United States] has brought a great fleet to Hawaii to show us that it's within striking distance of Japan means, conversely, that *we're* within striking distance too. In trying to intimidate us, America has put itself in a vulnerable position. If you ask me, they're just that bit too confident."[4] Admiral Richardson agreed: he did not believe the fleet was a deterrent by virtue of being at Pearl Harbor and warned Roosevelt that the fleet was not battle ready, especially for sustained operations west of Hawaii.

The decision to reinforce the Philippines reversed a policy that had written off their defense because of the long-standing judgment that the islands were certain to be quickly captured by the Japanese in the event of war. (The Philippines were 7,000 miles from the United States, but only about 1,000 miles from Japan and just 200 miles from Japanese-controlled Formosa.) As early as 1922, in the wake of the Washington Naval Treaty, which prohibited further fortification of the Philippines and effectively ceded naval domination of the Western Pacific to Japan, U.S. Navy planners had concluded that the Japanese could seize the Philippines and Guam before the U.S. Fleet could reach the Western Pacific. Japan was much closer than the United States to the Philippines, and by the end of 1940 Japanese forces had occupied Hainan Island and northern French Indochina, placing Japanese land-based air power within range of the American colony. The U.S. Army's leadership was also pessimistic about holding the Philippines, preferring a strategy of simply defending the Alaska-Hawaii-Panama triangle. There were no plans to reinforce the Philippines, and in the event of war the commander of the small Philippine-based U.S. Asiatic Fleet had the authority to decide whether to fight or withdraw to Hawaii or Singapore.[5] Roosevelt had long questioned the defensibility of the Philippines. Shortly after his first reelection in November 1936 he told Francis B. Sayre, whom he later appointed to the post of high commissioner to the Philippines, that a major U.S. naval base in the islands would "constitute a liability rather than an asset," and that "in case of a Japanese attack on the Philippines we would have to let the Philippines go temporarily and that we would be gradually be moving westward, making our position secure on one Pacific island after another as we slowly moved West."[6]

Though pessimism about the defensibility of the Philippines turned out to be well founded, it was not universal. On July 26, 1941, the same day Roosevelt froze Japanese assets in the United States, he also appointed retired U.S. Army Chief of Staff Douglas MacArthur to command all army forces in the Far East and called the Philippine Army into service of the United States. MacArthur was not at all convinced that the Philippines were indefensible. On the contrary, he soon came to believe that the islands, if reinforced, could be held; after all, *he* would command their defense. (The U.S. garrison in the Philippines rose from 8,563 troops to over 31,095 by the time the Japanese struck Pearl Harbor.[7]) For Stimson and Marshall, MacArthur's optimism seemed validated by reports (erroneous as it turned out) of the performance of a handful of U.S. long-range B-17s in service with the Royal Air Force against targets in German-occupied Europe. Stimson and Marshall convinced themselves that even a relatively small Philippines-based B-17 force could defend the islands and perhaps even deter a Japanese attack altogether.[8] In a letter to Roosevelt on October 21, 1941, Stimson declared that a "strategic opportunity suddenly arises in the Pacific Ocean. . . . Far from being impotent to influence events in that area, we suddenly find ourselves vested with the possibility of great effective power [which] if not promptly called by the Japanese, bids fair to stop Japan's march south and secure the safety of Singapore."[9] Stimson and Marshall even had fantastic visions of bombing Japan directly from the Philippines and of shuttle bombing Japan back and forth from the Philippines and bases in the Soviet Far East.[10] They seemed oblivious to two facts: first, Japan lay beyond the combat radius of B-17s based in the Philippines; and second, that Stalin, reeling from Hitler's invasion of the Soviet Union, would have been insane to have invited war with Japan. (Additionally, they could not have known how ineffective B-17s would prove as high-altitude bombers of moving naval targets.) According to the U.S. Army's official history of the war:

it was the airmen's argument that their long-range bomber, the B-17, could do what the Navy could not that convinced the more skeptical and paved the way for a new view of the defense of the Philippines. A force of these bombers based in the Philippines, it was contended, would not only serve to defend the islands but it would constitute such a threat to Japanese movements southward toward the Netherlands Indies as to deter Japan from further aggression in that region. [11]

By the end of September, reinforcements—troops, tanks, artillery, fighter aircraft, and B-17s—were flowing into the Philippines in the hope that they would have "a profound strategic effect in a Pacific conflict and might well be the decisive element in deterring Japan from opening hostilities."[12] Completion of planned reinforcements, which included 165 to 170 B-17s, was scheduled for March 1942, and U.S. Army planners were prepared to risk the possibility that Japan would strike before then.

The Japanese were not impressed. They attacked the Philippines a few hours after Pearl Harbor and destroyed all but four of the islands' thirty-five B-17s on the ground. The hasty decision to build up U.S. forces in Southeast Asia "was a disastrous strategic miscalculation for the United States, because the belief that a scratch force of American bombers and a few British warships could be transformed into a 'big stick' that would force the Japanese to halt their advance southward was a gamble doomed to failure," contends Edwin Layton. On the contrary, by "embarking on a deterrent policy before the military forces were installed in the Philippines to make it credible, Britain and the United States succeeded in making the concept of a preemptive strike an attractive option to the Japanese."[13]

Obviously, the United States failed to deter the Japanese, who preferred the horrendous risks of war with the United States over a humiliating retreat from empire. Those within the Roosevelt administration who believed the Japanese would not go to war with the United States were wrong. So too were those who believed the United States could deter a Japanese advance into Southeast Asia via such measures as a significant "forward" U.S. naval presence in Hawaii, economic sanctions, and B-17s in the Philippines. The United States sought to stop Japan without a war, but ended up provoking war.

Significantly, at no point in 1941 did Roosevelt threaten war; he did not want war with Japan, and he undoubtedly recognized that "[n]o unequivocal warning could be given" because he "could not be sure of American reaction in the event of actual crisis." Roosevelt was "fully aware of the need to secure congressional approval for war, the strength of isolationist sentiment in the United States, and of the difficulties [of] demonstrating that a [Japanese] attack on British and Dutch colonies [in Southeast Asia] was a direct threat [to] American interests."[14] By the fall of 1941 the president was also focused on Britain's struggle against Nazi Germany and its attendant undeclared U.S.-German shooting war in the North Atlantic; Japan could be taken care of later, after the war in Europe had been decided. The U.S. Navy's leadership, whose advice Roosevelt, a former assistant secretary of the navy, routinely consulted, was strongly opposed to any U.S. measures that might provoke war with Japan. A navy War Plans Division assessment completed just days before Roosevelt's imposition of the oil embargo, concluded that a U.S. shut-off of oil deliveries to Japan would provoke a Japanese invasion of the Dutch East Indies that would include military action against the Philippines.[15] The navy had its hands full in the Atlantic; it was in no position to challenge Japan's naval dominance east of Pearl Harbor. "It has long been my opinion that Germany cannot be defeated unless the United States is wholeheartedly in the war and makes a strong military and naval effort wherever strategy dictates," wrote Admiral Stark in an October memorandum to Secretary of State Cordell Hull. "It would be very desirable to enter the war under circumstances in which Germany were the aggressor and in which case Japan might then be able to remain neutral. However, on the whole, it is my opinion that the United States should enter the war as soon as possible, even if hostilities with Japan must be accepted."[16]

Yet if the administration was prepared to go to war over a Japanese advance into Southeast Asia, it should have made that fact plain to Tokyo. At the Placentia Bay Conference of August 1941, from which the

Atlantic Charter was proclaimed, the British proposed identical parallel Anglo-American declarations to Tokyo, warning that "Any further encroachment by Japan in the Southwestern Pacific would produce a situation in which the United States Government [and His Majesty's Government] would be compelled to take counter measures *even though these might lead to war* between the United States [, Great Britain,] and Japan."[17] Churchill did not believe there was much chance of stopping Japanese aggression in Southeast Asia short of a clear-cut threat of war by the United States and Great Britain, but was unprepared to issue such a threat except in conjunction with Roosevelt. Roosevelt, however, was unwilling to go that far. Yet it was

> never clear what progressive economic pressure and the retention of the Pacific Fleet at Pearl Harbor were supposed to do. Roosevelt did not intend these as measures preparatory for actual war; he did want them to restrain Tokyo. But if the United States meant to deter Japan from taking steps regarded as threatening, it ought to have been issuing far clearer warnings, as the amazement of Tokyo at the asset freeze attests. If Washington hoped to hinder Japan's ability to make war whether as a hedge in case conflict came or to block the conquest of the southwestern Pacific and capitulation of Chiang's regime [in China], gradual pressure was a poor road to take.[18]

Cordell Hull conceded after the war that by the beginning of 1941 "Japan knew that our economic pressure was growing," but what "Japan did not know was whether and in what circumstances we would use force."[19] Perhaps the Japanese would not have been deterred from war even had Roosevelt publicly declared that the United States would use force to oppose any Japanese attack in Southeast Asia. But we will never know because neither Roosevelt nor Hull credibly threatened the use of force.

Ambassador Grew had anticipated the possibility of unthreatened or vaguely threatened force seven months before Roosevelt froze Japanese assets in the United States. In his December 1940 letter to Roosevelt, Grew warned that

It is important to constantly bear in mind the fact that if we take measures "short of war" with no real intention to carry these measures to their final conclusion if necessary, such a lack of intention will be all too obvious to the Japanese, who will proceed undeterred, and even with greater incentive, on their way. Only if they become certain that we mean to fight if called upon to do so will our preliminary measures stand some chance of proving effective and of removing the necessity for war. [20]

In postwar testimony Grew elaborated. "I took the position" that because "economic embargoes in the nature of sanctions . . . are always interpreted as international insults . . . we should not place embargoes on Japan unless we were prepared to go all the way through with whatever might result from [them]."[21]

A few days before the attack on Pearl Harbor, Roosevelt *did* make a solid though secret pledge to the British ambassador in Washington that the United States would go to war in response to a Japanese attack on British or Dutch territory in Southeast Asia, a pledge that capped increasingly firm verbal assurances beginning in July.[22] Roosevelt had believed, at least since the formation of the so-called Axis alliance (the Tripartite Pact), that Japan and Germany were closely coordinating their agendas of aggression. (They were not. The Germans did not inform the Japanese of their planned attack on the Soviet Union, with which Japan had recently signed a non-aggression pact, and the Japanese did not alert the Germans to their planned attack on Pearl Harbor.) Roosevelt also believed, as we have seen, that the survival of Britain's empire in Asia was essential to Britain's ability to continue fighting Germany and Italy in Europe. Yet he never indicated to anyone, including the British ambassador, how he thought he could obtain a declaration of war against Japan in response to a Japanese advance into Southeast Asia limited to European colonies. What if the Japanese had attacked only Malaya, Singapore, and the Dutch East Indies, leaving the Philippines and Hawaii alone? Could Roosevelt have persuaded Congress to go to war on behalf of European colonies in Asia? (On August 12 the House of Representatives had voted to extend the Selective Service Act by a single vote; but for that one vote, the U.S. Army would have largely disintegrated.) Roosevelt speechwriter Robert Sherwood, who believed that Roosevelt and General George Marshall "were far more afraid of the isolationists at home . . . than they were of the enemies abroad,"[23] described Roosevelt's dilemma in his Pulitzer Prize–winning biography of Roosevelt and Harry Hopkins:

> The Japanese were about to strike at British or Dutch possessions or both—and what could we do about it? The British and the Dutch were hopelessly unable to defend themselves and so were the exposed Dominions of Australia and New Zealand. . . . Without formidable American intervention, the Japanese would be able to conquer and exploit an empire, rich in resources, stretching from the Aleutian Islands to India or even to the Middle East; and it was idle to assume, and Roosevelt knew it better than anyone else, that there could be any formidable American intervention without the full, final, irrevocable plunging of the entire nation into war. And what were the chances of that [if the Japanese struck only the British and the Dutch]? What would the President have to say to the Congress in that event? . . . Why . . . should Americans die for . . . such outposts of British imperialism as Singapore or Hong Kong or of Dutch imperialism in the East Indies?[24]

Hopkins recalled several talks with Roosevelt during the year before Pearl Harbor in which Roosevelt expressed concern that "the tactics of the Japanese would be to avoid conflict with us; that they would not attack either the Philippines or Hawaii but would move on Thailand, French Indo-China [and] make further inroads on China itself and attack the Malay Straits." Hopkins then recalled Roosevelt's subsequent "relief" that the Japanese had attacked U.S. territory. "In spite of the disaster at Pearl Harbor and the blitz-warfare with the Japanese during the first few weeks, it completely solidified the American people and made the war upon Japan inevitable."[25] The army's official history of the war concludes that

Perhaps the major error of the Japanese was their decision to attack the United States when the main objective was to gain the strategic resources of Southeast Asia. Had they bypassed the Philippines and rejected Yamamoto's plan for a strike against Pearl Harbor, it is possible that the United States might not have gone to war, or, if it had, that the American people would have been more favorably disposed toward a negotiated peace. While the Japanese would have had to accept certain risks in following such a course, they would not have forced the United States to declare war. [26]

A Japanese attack on *American* territory *somewhere* in the Pacific was the only event that could elicit a congressional declaration of war, and Roosevelt, unlike later presidents, respected the Congress's constitutional prerogative to declare war. It was also necessary that the attack appear unprovoked to the American people. Stimson testified in 1946 that such an attack was necessary to unite the country behind any war with Japan. Even though by late November 1941 the administration knew that a Japanese attack was coming (a "war warning" was issued on November 27 to all U.S. Army and Navy commanders), and "[i]n spite of the risk involved . . . in letting the Japanese fire the first shot," said Stimson, "we realized that in order to have the full support of the American people it was desirable to make sure that the Japanese be the ones to do this so that there should remain no doubt in anyone's mind as to who were the aggressors." [27]

Luckily for the Roosevelt administration, the Japanese obliged. Japanese leaders had come to regard war with the United States as both inevitable and—after the imposition of the oil embargo—urgent, and they seemed completely oblivious to the domestic political difficulties they might have caused Roosevelt had they confined their attacks in Southeast Asia to British and Dutch possessions. The IJN in particular insisted that the United States and Great Britain were strategically inseparable (mirroring Roosevelt's view of Germany and Japan) and that an attack on the British and the Dutch in Southeast Asia was sure to provoke a violent U.S. response, and therefore that it was imperative to preempt the United States militarily.

Unluckily for the administration, war with Japan might well have been avoided but for an unwillingness—in an age of Western territorial empires—to accept the legitimacy of any Japanese imperial ambitions in East Asia (outside Korea), and but for a failure to appreciate Tokyo's probable response to economic sanctions that threatened to eliminate Japan as a respectable industrial and military power. A refusal to accept some measure of Japanese hegemony in Manchuria and North China (as the Japanese accepted America's self-proclaimed hegemony in the Western Hemisphere) precluded a negotiated settlement that might have enabled the Roosevelt administration to concentrate U.S. attention and resources on the Nazi German threat in Europe that it rightly regarded as far more dangerous than Japanese aggression in East Asia. And by airily jerking its lethal economic leash around Japan's neck to punish Tokyo for aggression that Washington was never prepared to resist by force—or even threatened force—the Roosevelt administration invited the very war in the Far East it sought to avoid. "Instead of complementing his Europe-first strategy and orientation, the oil embargo threatened to disorient and distract [Roosevelt] from what he conceived to be his primary task by forcing Japan to consider war," conclude David Klein and Hilary Conroy.[28] Roland Worth Jr. contends that "the U.S. decision to embargo 90 percent of Japan's petroleum and two-thirds of its trade led directly to the attack on Pearl Harbor." Although "striking at the economic Achilles Heel of Japan was naturally appealing in light of its economy's comparative weakness, it only made sense if one were genuinely ready to negotiate a mutually acceptable compromise (which meant leaving Japan a good part of its empire) or if one were willing to risk the military retaliation that Japan . . . was quite capable of inflicting."[29] Bruce Russett agrees: "The Japanese attack would not have come but for the . . . embargo on the shipment of strategic materials to Japan. . . . Either raw material supplies had to be restored by a peaceful settlement with the Western powers, or access to the resources in Thailand, Malaya, and the Indies would have to be secured by force while Japan still retained the capabilities to do so."[30] The late historian John Toland, in his best-selling *The Rising Sun: The Decline and Fall of the Japanese Empire*, concluded that

America made a grave diplomatic blunder by allowing an issue not vital to her basic interests—the welfare of China—to become, at the last moment, the keystone of her foreign policy. Until that summer [of 1941] America had two limited objectives in the Far East: to drive a wedge between Japan and Hitler, and to thwart Japan's southward thrust. She could easily have obtained both these objectives but instead made an issue out of no issue at all, the Tripartite Pact, and insisted on the liberation of China. . . . America could not throw the weight of her strength against Japan to liberate China, nor had she ever intended to. Her major enemy was Hitler. [The Pacific War was] a war that need not have been fought. [31]

Coercive diplomacy requires carrots as well as sticks, but the United States was never prepared to make any concessions to Japan, not even a temporary *modus vivendi*—for example, a return to the *status quo ante* before Japan's move into southern Indochina and the U.S. imposition of the oil embargo. Such a deal was actually proposed in late 1941 by Ambassador Nomura, a staunch opponent of war with America, and endorsed by Marshall and Stark as a means of affording the United States more time to strengthen U.S. defenses in the Pacific.[32] In the absence of any attempt to conciliate Japan on crucial issues, U.S. coercive diplomacy was doomed to fail. George C. Herring, in his majesterial history of American foreign policy, concludes that

Had the [United States] abandoned, at least temporarily, its determination to drive the Japanese from China and restored some trade, it might have delayed a two-front war when it was not yet ready to fight one major enemy. Having already learned what seemed the hard lessons of appeasement [in Europe], U.S. officials rejected a course of expediency. Rather, they backed a proud nation into a position where its only choices were war or surrender.[33]

Paul W. Schroeder, in his highly insightful 1958 study of the role of the Tripartite Pact in U.S.-Japanese relations during 1941, detected a major—and fateful—American policy departure: from containment of further Japanese expansion to a rollback of established Japanese con-

quests, including China. The administration was apparently embold-
ened by Hitler's invasion of Russia, which diverted most of Germany's
military power away from Great Britain and, at least initially, promised
to divert the Japanese northward, away from Southeast Asia. Roosevelt
may also have sought to deter a Japanese attack on Russia by taking a
tougher line with Tokyo. Whereas during the first half of 1941 the United States was still not prepared to go to war over China and was focused
instead on detaching Japan from the Tripartite Pact and thwarting a Japanese advance into Southeast Asia, during the second half Washington
escalated its objective to that of stripping Japan of its empire altogether.
Schroeder contended that the Roosevelt administration's imposition of
the embargo was moving Japan toward concessions on both the Tripartite Pact and the southward advance.

> The policy of the United States, meanwhile, underwent a corre-
> sponding change: America went on the diplomatic offensive after
> July 1941. Her aims were no longer simply those of holding the line
> against Japanese advances and of inducing Japan to draw away
> from an alliance which the United States considered menacing. The
> chief objective of American policy was now to push Japan back, to
> compel her to withdraw from her conquests. . . . The objective that
> had previously been the least important and pressing in American
> policy, the liberation of China, now became the crucial consider-
> ation. American diplomats made a prompt and total evacuation of
> Japanese troops the *sine qua non* for agreement. [34]

The demand for China's evacuation was not just unacceptable to
Japan and therefore a diplomatic dead end. For the United States it
was also strategically nonsensical. The whole point of U.S. assistance to
Chiang Kai-shek was to tie down as many Japanese troops in the Chinese
quagmire as possible; Japanese troops in China were troops unavailable
for military operations elsewhere. A Japanese withdrawal from China
would release large armies for an invasion of Southeast Asia, Siberia, or
both. The demand for evacuation placed U.S. diplomacy at odds with
U.S. strategic interests.

As late as November 1941, Roosevelt himself was interested in exploring the possibility of a modus vivendi with Japan. He apparently suggested the idea to Hull because on November 11 the State Department's Far East Division drafted a memorandum that became the basis of later discussion of a possible diplomatic and military truce with Japan. According the memorandum, the purpose of such a truce was to buy sufficient time to work out "an eventual comprehensive settlement [with Japan] of a nature compatible with our principles."[35] In an undated note submitted to Hull probably on or about November 17 Roosevelt laid out his ideas on a temporary (six months) deal with Japan:

1) U.S. to resume economic relations—some oil and rice now—more later.
2) Japan to send no more troops to Indo-China or Manchurian border or any place south (Dutch, Brit. or Siam).
3) Japan to agree not to invoke tripartite pact if U.S. gets into European war.
4) U.S. to *introduce* Japs to Chinese to talk things over but U.S. take no part in their conversations.
Later on Pacific agreements.[36]

Roosevelt clearly sought to buy time in the Pacific, and the memorandum's last sentence suggests that he did not dismiss the possibility of a comprehensive settlement of some kind. The memorandum ignored the issue of a Japanese military evacuation of China or even of Indochina, and though it was not clear what Roosevelt meant by diplomatically "introducing" the Japanese to the Chinese, he clearly intended that the United States encourage a negotiated settlement of the Japanese war in China.

The State Department modified Roosevelt's proposals by reducing the proposed truce to ninety days, mandating the withdrawal of all Japanese troops from southern Indochina, and insisting on a more restricted lifting of the embargo. In the end, however, Hull dropped the modus vivendi proposal because of predictably strong opposition from China and tepid responses from Britain and Australia. Hull also believed the Japanese would certainly reject it because, as he testified after the war, "it contained only a little chicken feed in the shape of some cotton, oil, and a few other commodities in very limited quantities as compared with the unlimited quantities the Japanese were demanding."[37] But it was the potential impact on China that was decisive. "The Chinese Government violently opposed the idea," recounted Hull. "[T]he conclusion with Japan of such an arrangement would have been a major blow to Chinese morale. In view of these considerations it became clear that . . . the modus vivendi did not warrant assuming the risks involved with proceeding with it, especially the serious risk of collapse of Chinese morale and resistance [to the Japanese]."[38] "Once again, at a crucial juncture," observed Paul Schroeder, "the China issue had shown itself to be decisive."[39]

American public opinion also could not be ignored. Roosevelt surely understood that a modus vivendi with Japan at so late a date would be widely regarded as a morally outrageous act of appeasement completely at odds with the U.S. policy of strident intervention in Europe. How could one justify leaning so far forward toward war against Hitler while simultaneously seeking to propitiate Hitler's sole ally in Asia? Had not the harsh lessons of appeasement already been learned in Europe? An electorate that had been led to believe that the Axis Powers were morally and strategically indivisible would not understand a policy of intervention in Europe and appeasement in Asia, especially against an enemy that was viscerally more detested than the Germans. Langer and Gleason pointed out that "even the most responsible newspapers were dinning into the ears of the Administration the impossibility and immorality of any retreat from its established position vis-à-vis Japan, or of any settlement made at the expense of China."[40] A modus vivendi also would have been anathema to Stimson, Morgenthau, and other key members of Roosevelt's cabinet who had long pushed for a hard line against Japan. Roosevelt, in short, "would have had to contend against the very elements of public life which he had most strongly supported in his interventionist policy toward Europe."[41] Though Roosevelt, Marshall, and Stark were attracted by the practical arguments for a modus vivendi— i.e., that it would permit the United States to continue its primary strategic focus on Europe, even for a few more months, and buy additional time to strengthen U.S. defenses in the Pacific—even a temporary compromise with Japan would have been an exceptionally hard political sell to the American public and might even have demoralized the Nationalist Government in China to the point of ceasing resistance to accepting Tokyo's control of the real estate Japan had already conquered in China. Mark Stoler has argued that

> even a temporary agreement could wreck the coalition [Roosevelt] had been building to oppose further Japanese aggression. Equally if not more important, such a temporary agreement could also wreck the domestic support he had been building for aid to Britain and hostilities against Germany, since it asked the public to accept, albeit temporarily, the appeasement of Japan at the same time he was asking it to accept his opposite conclusion that appeasement of Germany had been a mistake and that the nation should now risk war in the Atlantic to reverse that mistake. Moreover, reaching an agreement with Japan would not only mean the end of an independent China, but also free Japanese military forces to attack the Soviet rear in Siberia. [42]

Schroeder nevertheless believed that U.S. policy from July to December of 1941 "was a grave mistake" because it overthrew the longstanding position "that the United States would not go to war for the sake of China."[43] Schroeder contended that by insisting on a Japanese military evacuation of China and employing extreme economic pressure to force the Japanese out, "the United States was carrying out a new offensive policy which made the crucial difference between peace and war."[44] Thus for Japan, "the attack [on Pearl Harbor] was an act of desperation, not madness. Japan fought only when she had her back to the wall as a result of America's diplomatic and economic offensive."[45] As for cutting a temporary political truce with Japan in late 1941, Schroeder argued that

> A limited *modus vivendi* agreement would not have required the United States in any way to sanction Japanese aggression or to abandon her stand on Chinese [territorial] integrity and indepen-

dence. It would have constituted only a recognition that the American government was not then in a position to enforce its principles, reserving for America full freedom of action at some later, more favorable time. Nor would it have meant the abandonment and betrayal of China. Rather it would have involved the frank recognition that the kind of help the Chinese wanted was impossible for the United States to give at that time. [46]

If the United States failed to deter Japan, so too did the Japanese fail to deter the United States. The failure of deterrence was mutual. Japan's adherence to the Tripartite Pact and subsequent increased belligerence in East Asia did not deter the Roosevelt administration from providing financial and military assistance to Chiang Kai-shek, using Tokyo's economic dependence on U.S. exports as a weapon, and reinforcing the Philippines. On the contrary, the harder Japan pushed, the harder the administration pushed back. The decision at the Imperial Conference of July 2, 1941, to advance into Southeast Asia even at the risk of war with the United States and Great Britain was a confession of failed deterrence. The Roosevelt administration certainly did not wish to be drawn into simultaneous wars in the Asia-Pacific and the Europe-Atlantic areas, but neither was it prepared, for fear of a two-front war, to accept Germany's conquest of Europe or Japan's conquest of East Asia. With respect to Japan at least, the United States was essentially undeterrable because the American homeland was invulnerable and because Americans never doubted the outcome of a war with Japan. Americans knew they could whip Japan, and they were not about to be intimidated by a despised aggressor state that had been terrorizing the helpless Chinese for years.

If anything staid Roosevelt's hand, it was isolationist sentiment at home. That historic sentiment was especially strong in the Congress, and Roosevelt, who sought to educate public opinion, was nonetheless careful, on foreign policy, not to get too far out in front of what he thought the domestic political traffic would bear. Roosevelt believed a showdown with Hitler was not only unavoidable but necessary, and by late 1941 had slowly nudged the United States out of the shackling neutrality legislation of the mid-1930s into a de facto military alliance with Great Britain and an undeclared shooting war with German submarines in the North Atlantic. He wanted war with Germany, not with Japan, but still could not have obtained a congressional declaration of war against either. The Japanese attack on Pearl Harbor and Hitler's subsequent declaration of war on the United States solved Roosevelt's problem and dealt a fatal blow to the survival of traditional American isolationism. But the strategic price for war with Germany was a simultaneous war with Japan.

CHAPTER SIX

Was the Pacific War Inevitable?

Japan's imperial ambitions in East Asia inexorably collided with Western interests in the region, and Japan's alliance with Nazi Germany, though of little operational significance, further alienated the Western powers. The Pacific War arose out of Japan's aggression in Southeast Asia, which was presaged by its occupation of southern Indochina in July 1941. Had Tokyo confined its aggression to Northeast Asia, it almost certainly could have avoided war with Britain and the United States, neither of which was prepared to go to war over China. The U.S. insistence, after Japanese forces moved into southern Indochina, that Japan evacuate *China* as well as Indochina, as a condition for the restoration of trade relations, thus made no sense as a means of dissuading the Japanese from moving south. On the contrary, the demand that Japan quit China killed any prospect of a negotiated alternative to Japan's conquest of Southeast Asia (e.g., restored trade in exchange for Japan's withdrawal from Indochina). In effect, *the United States went to war over China rather than Southeast Asia*—a volte-face of enormous strategic consequence since it propelled the United States into a war with Japan over a remote country for which the United States, with good reason, had never been prepared to fight. The fate of China did not engage core U.S. security interests, especially at a time when Europe's fate hung in the balance. A war with Japan was, of course, a war the United States was always going to win, but Japan was not the enemy the Roosevelt administration wanted to fight. The United States could have settled its accounts with Japan after Hitler's defeat had been assured.

That said, war with Japan at some point would have remained likely, even had the United States not insisted on Japan's military evacuation of China but instead offered Tokyo a modus vivendi along the lines Roosevelt outlined in his memorandum of mid-November 1941. At best, a modus vivendi would have been a temporary truce. By late 1941 the clash between core Japanese and U.S. security interests (in Southeast Asia) had become irreconcilable by means short of war. Japan was bent on further aggression, and the United States was determined to resist it. The United States was simply not prepared to accept Japan's conquest of the entire Far East, especially the strategically critical region of Southeast Asia. "It is true," observes Andrew Gordon, a Harvard history professor and director of the Reischauer Institute of Japanese Studies, "that the American moves to block Japan's advances in 1940 and 1941 confirmed the views of those in Japan who saw war as inevitable," and that for this reason, "some historians blame the Americans for taking steps that led to war." However,

> it is difficult to argue that a different American response would have avoided war. If the Americans had responded in a conciliatory fashion, the logic of expansionism would almost surely have led the Japanese military to view this as weakness and take further aggressive steps. Japanese rulers were blind to the possibility that others would not bend to their will. Beginning in 1931, they consistently responded to tension on the borders of the empire by pushing forward rather than standing in place or stepping back. Insofar as tensions were virtually inevitable, the invasion of Manchuria set in motion a chain of events that inexorably led to war. [1]

Michael Bess contends that

> In the end, it may not have made much difference if the United States had adopted a more conciliatory policy between 1939 and 1941. By that point, Japan was being led by men who would have

interpreted any such act of conciliation as weakness, as a sign that they could further step up their imperialist aggression. Sooner or later, the United States would have had to draw the line—or acquiesce in the emergence of a vast Asian military bloc dominated from Tokyo by a brutal and expansionist leadership. It is not reasonable to expect the United States to have stood by indefinitely, allowing such a clearly threatening development to continue unopposed.[2]

The roots of Japan's decision for war with the United States were economic and reputational. The termination of U.S. trade with Japan that followed Roosevelt's freezing of Japanese assets in July 1941 threatened to destroy Japan economically and militarily. A small, resource-poor, and overpopulated island state, Japan in the 1930s sought economic self-sufficiency and great power status via the acquisition of empire—just as Great Britain had done. (The United States could preach about the evils of imperialism and "spheres of influence" because as a huge, resource-rich, continental state it had no need for an overseas colonial empire; nor was its hegemony in the Western Hemisphere effectively challenged by other great powers. Indeed, as we have seen, the Japanese viewed the Monroe Doctrine as justification for their imperial ambitions.) Pyle, in his masterful assessment of modern Japan's behavior in the evolving international system, identifies "a persistent obsession with status and prestige—or, to put it in terms Japanese would more readily recognize, rank and honor."[3] From the time of the Meiji Restoration in 1868, "Japan strove and struggled for status as a great power. Other countries in Asia were aware of their backwardness, but nowhere else was this awareness so intense and so paramount that it drove a people with such single-minded determination. It became a national obsession to be the equal of the world's great powers."[4] A fusion of state-centered honor and popular nationalism occurred in Japan that prompted "an instinctive need for recognition of its status in the hierarchy of nations, and the values of hierarchy provided a behavioral norm that focused and intensified the realist drive for national power. Establishment of Japan's honor, of its reputation for power in relation to other nations, became a goal sanctioned by inherited values and norms."[5]

Yet the result of this drive for power, honor, and reputation was Japan's complete destruction and subsequent occupation by the United States. There can be no justification for a foreign policy that consciously propels a state into a war against an inherently undefeatable enemy. By the late 1930s a fatal abyss had opened between Japan's imperial ambitions and its material capacity to fulfill them. Japan simply did not have the resources to police Korea and Manchuria, conquer China, invade Southeast Asia, and defeat the United States in the Pacific. Japan lacked the necessary industrial strength, and what modest manufacturing base it did possess was critically dependent on imported oil and other commodities from the United States. Indeed, Japan's expanding war on the Asian mainland made it more dependent on imported U.S. commodities and finished goods. Japanese leaders refused to recognize the limits of Japan's power, despite the warnings of Nomohan and a continuing war in China they could never bring to a satisfactory conclusion. The very fact that Japanese leaders would consider sequential wars with the United States and the Soviet Union at a time when Japan was already militarily overstretched in China testifies to a fatal blindness to the strategic necessity of maintaining some reasonable harmony between political ambitions and military capacity. Like the Germans in both world wars, the Japanese seemed to believe that superior prowess at the operational level of war could and would—somehow—redeem reckless strategic decisions.[6] And again like the Germans, the Japanese, in the celebration of their own nationalism, were utterly insensitive to the nationalism of others.

Honor may have dictated the Japanese decision for war in 1941, but "suicide before dishonor" was a policy choice the Japanese might have avoided had Tokyo been willing and able to temper its imperial ambitions and accept some measure of economic dependence on the United States. For Japan, the prosperous and relatively democratic 1920s and the postwar decades as an economic powerhouse and ally of the United States demonstrate twentieth-century possibilities other than the path of autarky through aggression. The 1930s and 1940s were a tragic and, for Japan's victims, murderous detour from what might have been—and later was. For Japan in the twentieth century, good relations with the

United States were always a prerequisite for a secure Japan, whereas war with the United States was always going to be a disaster.

Still, it cannot be denied that, in threatening Japan's economic destruction (and consequent military impoverishment), the United States placed the Japanese in a position in which the only choices open to them were war or subservience. "Never inflict upon another major military power a policy which would cause you yourself to go to war unless you are fully prepared to engage that power militarily," cautions Roland Worth Jr. in his *No Choice but War: The United States Embargo Against Japan and the Eruption of War in the Pacific.* "And don't be surprised that if they do decide to retaliate, that they seek out a time and a place that inflicts maximum harm and humiliation upon your cause."[7] Roosevelt called the Japanese attack on Pearl Harbor "unprovoked." Was it?

Might the Pacific War have been avoided altogether? Was there a comprehensive political settlement acceptable to both Tokyo and Washington? What might such a settlement have looked like? In mid-November 1941 Secretary of the Treasury Henry Morgenthau drafted a proposed settlement of U.S.-Japanese issues that, had it been offered and accepted by Japan, would have removed any convincing cause for war in the Pacific, thereby permitting the United States to concentrate its full attention and resources on the German threat in Europe and the Atlantic.[8] The Morgenthau draft called for the United States to: (1) withdraw the bulk of its naval forces from the Pacific; (2) sign a twenty-year nonaggression treaty with Japan; (3) unfreeze Japanese assets; (4) restore most-favored-nation trade status to Japan; (5) extend to Japan a $2 billion credit at 2 percent for twenty years; (6) promote a final settlement of the Manchurian problem; (7) place Indochina under a joint commission composed of U.S., British, French, Chinese, and Japanese representatives, which would ensure most-favored-nation status of all five powers until the end of the European war; and (8) repeal, with the consent of Congress, those provisions of the Immigration Act of 1924 that excluded the immigration of Asians. In exchange for these concessions Japan would: (1) withdraw all of its military forces from China and Indochina; (2) discontinue support of any government in China other than that of Chiang Kai-shek—i.e., stop supporting rival puppet regimes; (3) sell to the United States up to three-quarters of its current war production on a cost-plus-twenty-percent basis; and (4) negotiate a ten-year nonaggression treaty with the United States, China, Britain, the Netherlands East Indies, and the Philippines.

In effect, the Morgenthau draft demanded that Japan disarm and abandon its empire as well as its alliance with Nazi Germany in exchange for a huge loan, restored trade with the United States on a most-favored-nation basis, and a reduction of U.S. naval power in the Pacific. Japan was asked to convert itself from a militarist aggressor state into a benign, demilitarized country whose economic security would be lodged in a liberal commercial relationship with the United States and Japan's East Asian neighbors. No Japanese government dominated by the Imperial Japanese Army could accept such terms. The Japanese militarists despised Western liberalism and valued empire and its expansion into Southeast Asia precisely because it offered an alternative to the very economic dependency on the United States that the Morgenthau draft sought to restore. The militarists were not going to renounce their political power or empire to please the United States. On the contrary, only a calamitous war with the United States could bring them down for good. And so it was.

CHAPTER SEVEN

The Enduring Lessons of 1941

The Japanese-American interaction of 1941 that led to war yields several enduring lessons of particular relevance to today's national security decision makers.

First, *fear and honor, "rational" or not, can motivate as much as interest.* The "realist" explanation of international politics as the struggle for power among calculating, self-interested states discounts fright, ideology, and pride as motivators of state behavior. Thucydides wrote that it was "the growth of the power of Athens, *and the alarm which this inspired in Sparta,* that made war inevitable" between the two city-states.[1] Clearly, it was the alarm inspired in Tokyo by the U.S. oil embargo—and the absence, in Japanese eyes, of an honorable alternative to war—that made the Pacific War inevitable by the end of 1941. Frightened national leaderships can behave recklessly, as can leaderships in the grip of powerful political or racial ideologies. The George W. Bush administration arguably overreacted to the horror of the 9/11 al Qaeda terrorist attacks by embracing torture as a means of extracting information from suspected terrorists and by invading and occupying Iraq, a country that had no link to the attacks. And it was Hitler's racial beliefs that propelled Nazi Germany into its fatal invasion of the Soviet Union. Honor can be no less a motivator—witness not only Japan's decision for war against the United States in 1941 but also Churchill's decision in 1940 to fight on after Dunkirk. France waged two fruitless wars in Indochina and Algeria because French leaders believed loss of empire would di-

minish France's prestige as a world power. For reasons of honor, the
American Confederacy, like the Japanese in World War II, fought on
long after any reasonable hope of victory had vanished. Gordon Prange
observed that the

Americans assumed, correctly, that Japan could not win a sustained
war against the United States. What they failed to consider was
one of the lessons of history: A so-called "have-not" nation may
well be possessed of a will and skill far out of proportion to her
resources. A later generation of Americans learned this the hard
way in Vietnam where, lacking the will to win, the U.S. suffered a
humiliating defeat.[2]

Japan's refusal to cut any of its losses in China or to countenance any
meaningful diplomatic concessions to the United States was the product
in large measure of an IJA leadership obsessed with its own reputation.
Indeed, that leadership seemed incapable of thinking outside the con-
fines of a narrowly conceived institutional self-interest, often confusing
the IJA's interests with that of the nation.

The phrase "prestige of the Army" (gun no ishin) runs like a fatal
thread through the history of the late 1920s and 1930s, becoming, in
time, the standard by which decisions affecting the whole course of
the nation's policy were taken. The proper function of any army—
defense of the nation—came to be overshadowed by the tendency
to think, or rather to feel, that the maintenance of the prestige of
the Army was a desirable goal in itself. This principle was carried
to extremes in Japan.[3]

The IJN was no less obsessed with its own prestige. Though Yamamoto and many other operational naval commanders were very pessimistic about Japan's prospects in a naval war with the United States,
the IJN as an institution could not openly admit, certainly not to the
emperor or to its great army rival, that it would likely lose a protracted
war with the U.S. Navy. To do so would undermine the decision for war
and suggest that the IJN lacked self-confidence. It would also raise the

question of why so much of Japan's resources had been poured into the IJN if it could not beat its only real competitor in the Pacific.[4]

Second, *there is no substitute for knowledge of a potential adversary's history and culture.* Mutual cultural ignorance was a major factor contributing to the outbreak of the Pacific War. With some notable exceptions like Ambassador Joseph Grew, American foreign policymakers knew little or nothing about Japan or the Japanese. On the Japanese side, there were some, like Admiral Yamamoto, who knew the United States well and respected American power and nationalism, but most Japanese leaders, especially senior IJA officers, knew little or nothing about America and Americans. Racial stereotypes prevailed on both sides, with the Americans, who had a long history of discrimination against racial minorities, including Japanese, believing the Japanese were a little yellow people incapable of waging war effectively against a modern Western power like the United States; and with the Japanese, who also regarded themselves as racially superior to their enemies, especially the Chinese, believing that the Americans were too materialistic and individualistic to muster the national discipline necessary for a long and bloody war. The Japanese were oblivious to the shock effect their attack on Pearl Harbor was certain to have on American public opinion.

Cultural ignorance continues to plague U.S. foreign policy. Americans proved to be as culturally ignorant of Vietnam and Iraq as they were of Japan, and it is testimony to that ignorance that the United States is probably the only modern country in the world where a person who speaks no foreign language can yet be considered well educated. The United States came to grief in Vietnam and Iraq because of a lack of knowledge of the two countries "best described as comprehensive and spectacular," observes Dennis Showalter.[5] Colin Gray convincingly argues that America's "strategic performance" is still hampered by cultural insensitivity:

> Bear in mind American public ideology, with its emphasis on political and moral uniqueness, manifest destiny, divine mission even, married to the multidimensional sense of national greatness. Such self-evaluation has not inclined Americans to be respectful of the beliefs, habits, and behaviors of other cultures. This has been, and

continues to be, especially unfortunate in the inexorably competitive field of warfare. From the Indian Wars on the internal frontier
to Iraq and Afghanistan today, the American way of war has suffered from the self-inflicted damage caused by failure to understand the enemy of the day. For a state that now accepts, indeed
insists upon, a global mandate to act as sheriff, this lack of cultural
empathy, including a lack of sufficiently critical self-knowledge, is
most serious. [6]

Third, *deterrence lies in the mind of the deterree, not the deterrer*. To be
effective, threatened force has to be credible *to the enemy*—i.e., the enemy
has to believe that you have both the capacity and the will to do what
you threaten to do, and that what you threaten to do is unacceptable to
the enemy. The Roosevelt administration attempted to deter a Japanese
military advance into Southeast Asia via a redeployment of powerful
U.S. naval forces to Hawaii, an imposition of escalating economic sanctions, and a military buildup in the Philippines. Key members of the
administration assumed that the Japanese could be deterred because—
surely—Tokyo knew it could not win a war with the United States. But
at no point along the road to Pearl Harbor did the administration clearly
threaten war; nor did it understand, until it was too late, that Tokyo preferred the risk of a lost war to a shameful peace. Though the imposition
of the oil embargo was clearly unacceptable to the Japanese, they opted
for war rather than submission. They were provoked, not deterred.

   That said, it is by no means clear that Japan would have been deterred by a clearly threatened U.S. use of force. How would the Japanese have responded to a public declaration by President Roosevelt on,
say, the day the United States froze Japanese assets, that any further
Japanese military move in Southeast Asia into territory not already under the control of Japan would mean war with the United States? How
credible would such a threat have been? The United States was strategically preoccupied with events in Europe and in no position militarily to
block a Japanese invasion of Southeast Asia. Additionally, the Roosevelt
administration's invocation of economic sanctions could be interpreted
as evidence of aversion to the use of force. Even today, economic sanctions are promoted as an alternative to force. Most importantly, most

Japanese leaders had, by July 1941, concluded that war with the United States was inevitable. Deterrence has little utility against an adversary that has concluded that war is unavoidable. The decision to launch a preventive war is prima facie evidence of failed deterrence.

America's crushing latent military superiority over Japan actually *encouraged* war because it made the passage of time a deadly enemy. Small though the possibilities of even a limited victory were in 1941, they would soon vanish altogether as the United States rearmed. Because the military balance was shifting irreversibly against Japan, Tokyo believed it had to initiate war as soon as possible to have a fighting chance.

The Japanese in 1941 prompt an additional observation about deterrence: an enemy prepared to run great risks might not be deterrable. The Japanese decision for war with the United States was an extraordinary gamble, and Admiral Nagano's declaration that it would be better to fight and lose than not to fight at all suggests an immunity to traditional deterrence. Like Hitler, the Japanese militarists were committed to an agenda of territorial conquest regardless of the risks incurred. Was a Japanese advance into Southeast Asia deterrable in the wake of the U.S. trade embargo? Indeed, did not the embargo simply accelerate the Japanese timetable? Deterrence theory presumes some measure of prudence on the part of the deterree, but perhaps the most striking aspects of the Liaison Conferences of 1941 are the refusal of any discussant to declare that Japan could win a war with the United States and the near complete absence of any discussion of the likely consequences of defeat. (There is, in contrast, no evidence that any American political or military leader in 1941 doubted the certainty of U.S. success in a war with Japan.)

Fourth, *strategy must always inform and guide operations.* The Japanese never had a coherent strategy for achieving their myriad objectives in China and Southeast Asia. This absence of strategy was attributable in part to the unbridgeable gap between Tokyo's ambitions in East Asia and its available military resources, and in part to the Japanese military's focus on the operational level of war. Kenneth Pyle has observed that for Japan to establish itself in the late 1930s as an East Asian hegemonic equivalent to the United States in the Western Hemisphere,

Japan needed military power sufficient for three major tasks—defeating the Soviet Army, whose strength on the borders of Manchuria had been vastly augmented; compelling the Chinese government to accept Japan's position in Manchuria and northern China; and securing the home islands against the U.S. fleet. These three objectives required a military capability Japan was never able to achieve. The Meiji leaders would have been appalled at the incautious ways in which the new leaders made policy commitments that exceeded the nation's capacities.[7]

The attack on Pearl Harbor was a crapshoot, a reckless roll of the dice with profound consequences which the Japanese may have sensed but never fully grasped, much less confronted, because Tokyo never had a strategy for defeating the United States. The Japanese never had a clear or convincing picture of how a war with the United States might end. They seemed to believe, or at least hope, that early operational successes would somehow deliver ultimate strategic success. One is reminded of the 2003 U.S. invasion of Iraq, especially the prewar lack of postwar planning and the mismatch between the amount of force employed and the war's objective of Iraq's political reconstruction. War planning focused almost exclusively on the destruction of the old regime through a swift conventional military campaign that would validate the effectiveness of "transformed" U.S. military forces. The Office of the Secretary of Defense sought a quick military victory and was oblivious to the potential force requirements for stabilizing post-Saddam Iraq. The apparent assumptions, at least among OSD's neoconservatives, were that Americans would be welcomed as liberators and that a stable democracy would naturally arise in Iraq once tyranny had been removed.

Fifth, *economic sanctioning is an inherently hostile act and can be tantamount to an act of war.* The economic sanctions the United States imposed on Japan in 1941 were probably the most ruinous of any in history short of wartime naval blockades. They were so destructive that the Japanese concluded they had no recourse but war. The damage that economic sanctions can inflict upon a state that is highly dependent on international trade can be equivalent to, if less dramatic than, an armed attack;

as such, they can provoke a violent reaction. The common view of economic sanctioning as an alternative to war needs to be reassessed, especially by the United States, which routinely sanctions regimes it does not like. Sanctioning is an inherently hostile act intended to coerce the sanctioned state to alter its behavior in some very important way, and today some states, such as Iran, have means of responding that avoid militarily challenging the United States head-on.

Paradoxically, sanctions can also be interpreted as evidence of weakness, i.e., an unwillingness or inability to use force. Enemies may read sanctions as proof of an aversion to war. In the case of the United States in the post–Cold War era, the relative popularity of sanctions, especially on Capitol Hill, lies precisely in the fact that they convey toughness without the risk of war. Key policymakers in the Roosevelt administration regarded sanctions as a substitute for war rather than an escalatory step toward war. Ambassador Grew was quite right to warn Roosevelt in December 1940 that the decision to impose draconian economic sanctions on Japan mandated a U.S. declaration that it was prepared to go further, i.e., use force, if the sanctions failed to deter further Japanese aggression. Failed or ignored sanctions can advertise impotence. For example, years of U.S. sanctioning of Iran and North Korea have deterred neither from continuing to pursue the acquisition of nuclear weapons, perhaps because they are not, like Iraq in 2003, militarily helpless, and perhaps because the United States has not credibly threatened the use of military force should sanctions fail. (How could it, given the dissipation of its military power in Iraq and Afghanistan?)

Sixth, *the presumption of moral or spiritual superiority can fatally discount the consequences of an enemy's material superiority.* Clausewitz was right: the best strategy is to be strong. The Japanese were hardly the last of America's enemies to believe that a superior willingness to fight and die could neutralize or even defeat U.S. advantages in firepower and technology. Mao Tse-tung convinced himself that the superior motivation and tactics of the People's Liberation Army could drive the Americans out of Korea, and other enemies, including Saddam Hussein (during the Persian Gulf crisis of 1990–1991) and Osama bin Laden, believed that the U.S. defeat in Vietnam and humiliation in Lebanon revealed an aversion to incurring casualties that could be decisively exploited. Facing a much stronger enemy can compel a belief in the offsetting superiority of one's own cause, race, or strategy and tactics. Indeed, irregular warfare offers the militarily weak perhaps the only chance of defeating the militarily strong, although most insurgencies fail precisely because they are simply too weak to win without ultimately developing a capacity for regular warfare. Mao Tse-tung himself regarded guerrilla warfare as a transition and complement to regular warfare. "The concept that guerrilla warfare is an end in itself and that guerrilla activities can be divorced from those of the regular forces is incorrect," he wrote in 1937. "[T]here can be no doubt that our regular forces are of primary importance, because it is they who are alone capable of producing the decision. Guerrilla warfare assists them in producing this favorable decision."[8] Mao had great respect for the conventional military superiority of his enemies, as did the Vietnamese Communists for that of the French and the Americans. The Vietnamese Communists employed regular military forces, not guerrillas, to defeat the French at Dien Bien Phu in 1954 and to overrun South Vietnam in 1975.

All that said, superior firepower and technology can and have been defeated by stronger political will and more effective strategy.[9] If it behooves the weak to respect the material superiority of the strong, the strong are well advised to recognize the limits of regular (conventional) warfare. The Pacific War may have been a war that Japan was always going to lose by virtue of its gross material inferiority to the United States, but Japan's decision for war with the United States and the ferocity of subsequent Japanese resistance in the Central and Southwestern Pacific testified to a defiant refusal to be intimidated by a country that dwarfed Japan in territory, population, natural resources, and industrial strength. More to the point, conventional military supremacy has limited utility against a determined enemy practicing protracted irregular warfare, especially if the possessor of that supremacy is a modern democracy characteristically self-restrained in the use of force and averse to incurring casualties on behalf of war aims that cannot sustain public support.[10] In Indochina the United States faced an enemy—North Vietnam and Communist forces in South Vietnam—that was materially far weaker relative to the United States than was Japan in 1941. Yet the Vietnamese Communists won because they were prepared to make far greater sacrifices proportional to their strength and because they relied primarily on a strategy of protracted irregular warfare that simultaneously sapped American political will and denied U.S. superiority in firepower and technology a decisive influence.

Seventh, *"inevitable" war easily becomes a self-fulfilling prophecy.* A war becomes inevitable when at least one side comes to believe it. Japan squandered a potentially decisive opportunity to avoid war with the United States by attacking only Europe's colonial possessions in Southeast Asia. Absent the attacks on Pearl Harbor and the Philippines, Roosevelt would have found it extremely difficult, perhaps even impossible, to carry the American electorate into war with Japan, and the Japanese might have gone on to secure the resources of the rest of Southeast Asia without arousing the armed wrath of the United States. By late summer of 1941, however, most Japanese leaders had come to regard war with the United States as unavoidable—and so it became as the Japanese moved to initiate it under the most favorable possible operational circumstances.

The assumption of inevitability encourages, even mandates, exploitation of the temporal opportunities of striking first, especially if the military balance with the enemy is shifting in his favor. Preventive war, which is not to be confused with preemptive military action to defeat a certain and imminent attack, rests upon the assumptions of inevitability and unfavorable strategic trends. The claim of inevitability also can be used to excuse or justify outright aggression. The George W. Bush administration believed, or at least publicly argued, that war with Saddam Hussein's regime was inevitable and that it was imperative to start that war before the Iraqi dictator acquired nuclear weapons. Unlike the Roosevelt administration, which mistakenly assumed (at least until 1941) that Japan was deterrable, the Bush administration assumed, or at least asserted, that a nuclear-armed Saddam Hussein would be undeterrable. It remains unclear whether proponents of war with Iraq really believed that war was inevitable and that Saddam was undeterrable. There was no persuasive prewar evidence that Iraq had a viable nuclear weapons program, but there was substantial evidence that Saddam was effectively deterred, and would have remained deterred, from using any weapon of mass destruction against the United States or U.S. forces in the Persian Gulf region.[11] What is clear is that the moral, strategic, and financial costs of the U.S. preventive war against Iraq have—so far—greatly exceeded the benefits claimed before the war by the Bush administration and its neoconservative supporters. (The substantial decline in insurgent and ethno-sectarian violence in 2007–2009 should not be mistaken for strategic victory. A definitive judgment on the U.S. decision to invade in 2003 must necessarily be shaped by what happens in and to Iraq after U.S. military forces depart, as they are scheduled to do by December 31, 2011. Middle East expert Steven Simon warns that the "surge [strategy] may have bought transitory success . . . but it has done so by stoking the three forces that have traditionally threatened the stability of Middle Eastern states: tribalism, warlordism, and sectarianism."[12])

The American experience in Iraq should serve as a warning to those who believe the United States should, if necessary, use force (or encourage Israel to use force) to prevent Iran from acquiring nuclear weapons. Some of the same neoconservative pundits and like-minded politicians who called for preventive war against Iraq have since called for war against Iran on the same discredited grounds that a nuclear-armed Iran would be undeterrable and that a war with that country, or at least its governing regime, is inevitable, and that it is better to have it before rather than after Teheran "goes nuclear." Yet short of an invasion and occupation of Iran, for which the United States simply lacks the necessary force (and political will), no military strike, even one based on exquisite intelligence, could promise anything other than a retardation of Iran's drive to acquire nuclear weapons. (The relevant lesson here is the 1981 Israeli air attack on Iraq's nuclear facility at Osirak, which simply reinforced Saddam's nuclear weapons ambitions and drove the Iraqi program literally underground.) Nor, despite the rantings of President Mahmoud Ahmadinejad, is there any convincing evidence that a nuclear-armed Iran would be undeterrable; Ahmadinejad is not the Iranian government's primary decision maker, and the evidence strongly suggests that Iran is seeking nuclear weapons for purposes of deterrence and prestige, not aggression.[13] (Indeed, what purposes, other than deterrence and prestige, do nuclear arsenals usefully serve?) Moreover, Iran, unlike Iraq in 2003, is not helpless; it could retaliate against U.S. forces in Iraq and oil tanker traffic in the Persian Gulf and foment terrorist attacks against American targets throughout the Middle East.

The negative consequences of a U.S. (or Israeli) strike against Iran, which almost certainly would strengthen the current regime's political grip on the country, would likely far outweigh any short-term benefits.[14] Indeed, attacking Iran could prove even more disastrous than the U.S. strategic blunder in Iraq:

> It would turn that country's oppressive leaders, who are now highly unpopular at home, into heroes of Islamic resistance; give them strong incentive to launch a violent counter-campaign against American interests around the world; greatly strengthen Iranian nationalism, Shiite irredentism, and Muslim extremism, thereby attracting countless new recruits to the cause of terror; undermine the democratic movement in Iran and destroy the prospects for political change there for at least another generation; turn the people of Iran, who are now among the most pro-American in the Middle East, into enemies of the United States; require the United States to remain deeply involved in the Persian Gulf indefinitely, forcing it to take sides in all manner of regional conflicts and thereby make a host of new enemies; enrage the Shiite-dominated government in neighboring Iraq, on which the United States is relying to calm the violence there; and quite possibly disrupt the flow of Middle East petroleum in ways that could wreak havoc on Western countries.[15]

Finally, Americans would do well to remember the disastrous long-term consequences, for the United States and Iran, of the last U.S. violent intervention in Iranian politics: the CIA-sponsored overthrow of the popular nationalist government of Prime Minister Mohammad Mossadegh in 1953.

Is the United States condemned to repeat in Iran its preventive war debacle in Iraq?

NOTES

Preface

1. Ernest R. May, "Conclusions," in *Knowing One's Enemies: Intelligence Assessment Before the Two World Wars* (Princeton, NJ: Princeton University Press, 1984), 520, italics in the original.

Chapter 1: Introduction: A "Strategic Imbecility"?

1. Winston Churchill, speech before a Joint Session of Congress, December 26, 1941, reprinted in *The War Speeches of Winston S. Churchill, 1939–1945*, Vol. 2, compiled by Charles Ead. 3 vols. (London: Cassell and Company, 1950), 150.

2. Quoted in Gordon W. Prange, with Donald M. Goldstein and Katherine V. Dillon, *Pearl Harbor: The Verdict of History* (New York: McGraw-Hill, 1986), 499.

3. Quoted in Louis Morton, *The War in the Pacific, Strategy and Command: The First Two Years* (Washington, DC: Center of Military History, U.S. Army, 1962), 125.

4. David J. Lu, *From the Marco Polo Bridge to Pearl Harbor: Japan's Entry Into World War II* (Washington, DC: Public Affairs Press, 1961), vii.

5. Quoted in Kenneth B. Pyle, *Japan Rising: The Resurgence of Japanese Power and Purpose* (New York: Public Affairs, 2007), 336.

6. Quoted in Jean Edward Smith, *FDR* (New York: Random House, 2007), 518.

7. Henry L. Stimson and McGeorge Bundy, *On Active Service in Peace and War* (New York: Harper and Brothers, 1948), 387.

8. Quoted in Sadao Asada, *From Mahan to Pearl Harbor: The Imperial Japanese Navy and the United States* (Annapolis, MD: Naval Institute Press, 2006), 276.

9. Quoted in ibid., 277.
10. Raymond Aron, *Peace and War: A Theory of International Relations* (New York: Doubleday and Company, 1966), 68, italics in the original.
11. Gordon W. Prange, *At Dawn We Slept: The Untold Story of Pearl Harbor* (New York: McGraw-Hill, 1981), 279.
12. Edward N. Luttwak, *Strategy: The Logic of War and Peace* (Cambridge, MA: Harvard University Press, 1987), 222.
13. Colin S. Gray, *War, Peace and International Relations: An Introduction to Strategic History* (New York: Routledge, 2007), 180, italics in the original.
14. Roberta Wohlstetter, *Pearl Harbor: Warning and Decision* (Palo Alto, CA: Stanford University Press, 1962), 355.
15. Toshikazu Kase, *Journey to the* Missouri (New Haven, CT: Yale University Press, 1950), 9.
16. Haruo Tohmatsu and H. P. Willmott, *A Gathering Darkness: The Coming of War to the Far East and the Pacific, 1921–1942* (Lanham, MD: SR Books, 2004), 1.
17. Robert B. Strassler, ed., *The Landmark Thucydides: A Comprehensive Guide to the Peloponnesian War* (New York: Free Press, 1996), Book 1, Chapter 76, 43.
18. B. H. Liddell Hart, *Strategy* (New York: Frederick A. Praeger, 1967), 269.
19. Norimitsu Onishi, "Japan Fires General Who Said a U.S. 'Trap' Led to Pearl Harbor," *New York Times*, November 1, 2003.
20. For assessments of the Yasukuni Shrine as both a domestic Japanese and an international political issue, see John Breen, ed., *Yasukuni: The War Dead and the Struggle for Japan's Past* (Singapore: Horizon Books, 2007).
21. Michael Bess, *Choices Under Fire: Moral Dimensions of World War II* (New York: Vintage Books, 2006), 32.
22. Ibid., 30.
23. See Jennifer Lind, "The Perils of Apology: What Japan Shouldn't Learn from Germany," *Foreign Affairs* 88, no. 3 (May/June 2009): 132–146.
24. Abraham Ben-Zvi, *The Illusion of Deterrence: The Roosevelt Presidency and the Origins of the Pacific War* (Boulder, CO: Westview Press, 1987), 78–80.
25. David Kahn, "The United States Views Germany and Japan in 1941," in *Knowing One's Enemies*, ed. May, 476–477.
26. Prange, *At Dawn We Slept*, 558.
27. Smith, *FDR*, 528.
28. See Alvin D. Coox, *Nomohan: Japan against Russia, 1939* (Palo Alto, CA: Stanford University Press, 1985), 1079–1090.
29. Prange, *At Dawn We Slept*, 35.

30. See the author's *The Wrong War: Why We Lost in Vietnam* (Annapolis, MD: Naval Institute Press, 1998), and *Dark Victory: America's Second War against Iraq* (Annapolis, MD: Naval Institute Press, 2004).
31. For an incisive account of the deliberations of the British cabinet during the crisis occasioned by Germany's defeat of the French army and the British Expeditionary Force in May 1940, see John Lukacs, *Five Days in London, May 1940* (New Haven, CT: Yale University Press, 1999), especially 104–161.
32. See Carlo D'Este, *Warlord: A Life of Winston Churchill at War* (New York: HarperCollins, 2008), 438–441; and David Reynolds, *In Command of History: Churchill Fighting and Writing the Second World War* (New York: Basic Books, 2005), 169–174.
33. Jonathan G. Utley, *Going to War with Japan, 1937–1941* (Knoxville: University of Tennessee Press, 1985), 157.
34. Prange, *At Dawn We Slept*, 372.

Chapter 2: Sources of Japanese-American Tension

1. U.S. Department of State, *Papers Relating to the Foreign Relations of the United States. Japan: 1931–1941*, Vol. 2 (Washington, DC: U.S. Government Printing Office, 1943), 383 (hereafter referred to as *FRUS—Japan 1931–1941* II).
2. Ibid., 543.
3. Harry Wray, "Japanese-American Relations and Perceptions, 1900–1941," in *Pearl Harbor Reexamined: Prologue to the Pacific War*, eds. Hilary Conroy and Harry Wray (Honolulu: University of Hawaii Press, 1990), 2.
4. Quoted in *Report on the Hearings before the Joint Committee on the Investigation of the Pearl Harbor Attack*, 79th Cong., 2nd sess. (Washington, DC: U.S. Government Printing Office, 1946), 9 (hereafter referred to as the *Pearl Harbor Attack Investigation Report*).
5. Joseph C. Grew, cable of December 17, 1934, reprinted in *Hearings before the Joint Committee on the Investigation of the Pearl Harbor Attack*, 79th Cong., 1st sess. (Washington, DC: U.S. Government Printing Office, 1946), Part 2, 565 (hereafter referred to as *Hearings on the Pearl Harbor Attack*).
6. George F. Kennan, *American Diplomacy* (Chicago: University of Chicago Press, 1951), 49.
7. Quoted in Margaret Macmillan, *Paris 1919: Six Months that Changed the World* (New York: Random House, 2001), 317–318.
8. For an examination of the Shantung issue at the Versailles Conference, see ibid., 322–344.
9. See Roger Daniels, *The Politics of Prejudice: The Anti-Japanese Movement in California and the Struggle for Japanese Exclusion* (Berkeley: University of California Press, 1977).

10. Pyle, *Japan Rising*, 132, 155.
11. Bess, *Choices Under Fire*, 21.
12. George C. Herring, *From Colony to Superpower: U.S. Foreign Relations Since 1776* (New York: Oxford University Press, 2008), 333.
13. Ibid.
14. Kennan, *American Diplomacy*, 37.
15. Ibid., 46.
16. Robert A. Divine, *The Reluctant Belligerent: America's Entry into World War II* (New York: John Wiley and Sons, 1965), 3.
17. *Pearl Harbor Attack Investigation Report*, 34.
18. Prange, *At Dawn We Slept*, 117–118.
19. Lu, *From the Marco Polo Bridge to Pearl Harbor*, 155.
20. Pyle, *Japan Rising*, 147, 148.
21. H. P. Willmott, *Empires in the Balance: Japanese and Allied Pacific Strategies to April 1942* (Annapolis, MD: Naval Institute Press, 1982), 38.
22. Quoted in Sadao Asada, "The Japanese Navy and the United States," in *Pearl Harbor as History: Japanese-American Relations, 1931–1941*, eds. Dorothy Borg and Shumpei Okamoto (New York: Columbia University Press, 1973), 237, italics in the original.
23. See David C. Evans and Mark C. Peattie, *Kaigun: Strategy, Tactics, and Technology in the Imperial Japanese Navy, 1887–1941* (Annapolis, MD: Naval Institute Press, 1997), 141–144.
24. Atsushi Oi, "The Japanese Navy in 1941," in *The Pacific War Papers: Japanese Documents on World War II*, eds. Donald M. Goldstein and Katherine V. Dillon (Washington, DC: Potomac Books, 2004), 12.
25. For discussions of Japanese naval strategy, see Stephen E. Pelz, *Race to Pearl Harbor: The Failure of the Second London Conference and the Onset of World War II* (Cambridge, MA: Harvard University Press, 1974), 34–39; and Hiiroyuki Agawa, *The Reluctant Admiral: Yamamoto and the Imperial Navy*, trans. by John Bester (Tokyo: Kodanshu International, 1979), 193–199.
26. H. P. Willmott, *The War with Japan: The Period of Balance, May 1942–October 1943* (Wilmington, DE: Scholarly Resources Books, 2002), xv.
27. Pelz, *Race to Pearl Harbor*, 2.
28. Ibid., 19.
29. Ibid., 197.
30. Ibid., 221.
31. Kichisaburo Nomura, "Japan's Demand for Naval Equality," *Foreign Affairs* (January 1935), 196.
32. Ibid., 198.
33. Ibid., 199.
34. Ibid., 202.
35. "Diary of Admiral Kichisaburo Nomura, June–December 1941," in *The Pacific War Papers*, eds. Goldstein and Dillon, 153.

36. Herring, *From Colony to Superpower*, 488–491.
37. Andrew J. Crozier, *The Causes of the Second World War* (Malden, MA: Blackwell, 1997), 192.
38. John W. Masland, "Missionary Influence Upon American Far Eastern Policy," *Pacific Historical Review* 10, no. 3 (September 1941): 280.
39. Henry L. Stimson, *The Far Eastern Crisis—Recollection and Observations* (New York: Harper Brothers, 1936), 153.
40. Masland, "Missionary Influence," 286, 287.
41. William L. Neumann, "Franklin D. Roosevelt and Japan, 1913–1933," *Pacific Historical Review* 22, no. 2 (May 1953): 152–153.
42. *FRUS—Japan: 1931–1941* II, 208–209.
43. William L. Langer and S. Everett Gleason, *The Undeclared War 1940–1941: The World Crisis and American Foreign Policy* (New York: Harper and Brothers, 1953), 296–305.
44. Lyman P. Van Slyke, "China," in *The Oxford Companion to World War II*, ed. I. C. B. Dear (New York: Oxford University Press, 1995), 211.
45. Prange, *Pearl Harbor: The Verdict of History*, 158.
46. *FRUS—Japan: 1931–1941*, II, 127.
47. Quoted in Paul W. Schroeder, *The Axis Alliance and Japanese-American Relations 1941* (Ithaca, NY: Cornell University Press, 1958), 121.
48. Quoted in Herbert Feis, *The Road to Pearl Harbor* (Princeton, NJ: Princeton University Press, 1950), 111.
49. Masuo Kato, *The Lost War: A Japanese Reporter's Inside Story* (New York: Alfred A. Knopf, 1946), 20.
50. Divine, *The Reluctant Belligerent*, 966–997.
51. *FRUS—Japan: 1931–1941*, II, 170.
52. Lu, *From the Marco Polo Bridge to Pearl Harbor*, 111.
53. Quoted in Langer and Gleason, *The Undeclared War*, 28.
54. Ibid., 26.
55. Schroeder, *The Axis Alliance*, 22.
56. Joseph C. Grew, *Turbulent Era: A Diplomatic Record of Forty Years, 1904–1941*, ed. Walter Johnson, Vol. 2 (Boston: Houghton Mifflin, 1952), 1231.
57. Schroeder, *The Axis Alliance*, 186.
58. *Hearings on the Pearl Harbor Attack*, Part 2, 558.
59. Quoted in *Pearl Harbor Attack Investigation Report*, 25.
60. Quoted in Lu, *From the Marco Polo Bridge to Pearl Harbor*, 119.
61. Kichisaburo Nomura, "Stepping-Stones to War," *U.S. Naval Institute Proceedings* (September 1951), 929.
62. Lu, *From the Marco Polo Bridge to Pearl Harbor*, 114.
63. Yale Candee Maxon, *Control of Japanese Foreign Policy: A Study of Civil-Military Rivalry 1930–1945* (Berkeley: University of California Press, 1957), 169.

64. Ian Nish, *Japanese Foreign Policy in the Interwar Period* (Westport, CT: Praeger, 2002), 168.
65. Letter from Roosevelt to Grew, January 21, 1941, *Hearings on the Pearl Harbor Attack*, Part 2, 632.
66. Quoted in Langer and Gleason, *The Undeclared War*, 19, italics in the original.
67. *FRUS—Japan: 1931–1941*, II, 139.
68. Ibid., 147.
69. Quoted in *Pearl Harbor Attack Investigation Report*, 17.
70. Langer and Gleason, *The Undeclared War*, 642.
71. Quoted in ibid., 644.
72. Quoted in ibid., 645.
73. Walter LaFeber, *The Clash: A History of U.S.-Japanese Relations* (New York: W. W. Norton, 1997), 182.
74. Cordell Hull, *The Memoirs of Cordell Hull* (New York: Macmillan, 1948), 637.
75. *Hearings on the Pearl Harbor Attack*, Part 2, 412.
76. *FRUS—Japan: 1931–1941*, II, 51.
77. H. W. Brands, *Traitor to His Class: The Privileged Life and Radical Presidency of Franklin Delano Roosevelt* (New York: Doubleday, 2008), 569.
78. For a detailed documentary history of U.S. sanctioning of Japan from 1939 to Pearl Harbor, see *FRUS—Japan: 1931–1941*, II, 189–273.

Chapter 3: Japanese Aggression and U.S. Policy Responses, 1937–1941
1. Kato, *The Lost War*, 40.
2. Ian Nish, *Japanese Foreign Policy in the Interwar Period*, 139–141.
3. Sachiko Murakami, "Indochina: Unplanned Incursion," in *Pearl Harbor Reexamined*, eds. Conroy and Wray, 148.
4. See Waldo Heinrichs, "The Russian Factor and Japanese-American Relations, 1941," in *Pearl Harbor Reexamined*, eds. Conroy and Wray, 163–177.
5. Ibid., 163.
6. Morton, *The War in the Pacific*, 97.
7. Jonathan Marshall, *To Have and Have Not: Southeast Asian Raw Materials and the Origins of the Pacific War* (Berkeley: University of California Press, 1995), 134.
8. *FRUS—Japan: 1931–1941*, II, 342.
9. Letter from Grew to Roosevelt, December 14, 1941, *Hearings on the Pearl Harbor Attack*, 631.
10. Harold Ickes, *The Secret Diary of Harold L. Ickes*, Vol. 3, *The Lowering Clouds 1939–1941* (New York: Simon and Schuster, 1965), 588.
11. James William Morley, ed., David A. Titus, trans., *Japan's Road to the Pacific War, The Final Confrontation: Japan's Negotiations with the United States, 1941* (New York: Columbia University Press, 1994), 5.

12. Langer and Gleason, *The Undeclared War*, 649.
13. Irvine H. Anderson Jr., "The 1941 *De Facto* Embargo on Oil to Japan: A Bureaucratic Reflex," *Pacific Historical Review* 44, no. 2 (May 1975): 202–203.
14. Edward S. Miller, *Bankrupting the Enemy: The U.S. Financial Siege of Japan before Pearl Harbor* (Annapolis, MD: Naval Institute Press, 2007), 162.
15. John McVickar Haight Jr., "Franklin D. Roosevelt and a Naval Quarantine of Japan," *Pacific Historical Review* 40, no. 2 (May 1971): 203–26.
16. Feis, *The Road to Pearl Harbor*, 109.
17. Ibid., 157; Miller, *Bankrupting the Enemy*, 120–123.
18. Michael A. Barnhart, *Japan Prepares for Total War: The Search for Economic Security, 1919–1941* (Ithaca, NY: Cornell University Press, 1987), 215.
19. Utley, *Going to War with Japan*, 126–132.
20. Ben-Zvi, *The Illusion of Deterrence*, 19–24.
21. Utley, *Going to War with Japan*, 126.
22. See Anderson, op. cit., and Miller, op. cit., 191–204.
23. See John Morton Blum, ed., *From the Morgenthau Diaries*, Vol. 2, *Years of Urgency, 1938–1941* (Boston: Houghton Mifflin, 1965), 348–359, 377–380.
24. Roland H. Worth Jr., *No Choice but War: The United States Embargo against Japan and the Eruption of War in the Pacific* (Jefferson, NC: McFarland and Company, 1995), 115–117.
25. Joseph C. Grew, *Ten Years in Japan: A Contemporary Record Drawn from the Diaries and Private and Official Papers of Joseph C. Grew* (New York: Simon and Schuster, 1944), 469.
26. Dean Acheson, *Present at the Creation: My Years in the State Department* (New York: W. W. Norton, 1969), 19.
27. Ben-Zvi, *The Illusion of Deterrence*, 67–76.
28. See Worth, *No Choice but War*, 197–199.
29. *FRUS—Japan: 1931–1941*, II, 527–528.
30. Ibid., 265.
31. See Anderson, "The *De Facto* Embargo," 202–3; and Conrad Black, *Franklin Delano Roosevelt: Champion of Freedom* (New York: Public Affairs, 2003), 652, 676.
32. See Ben-Avi, *The Illusion of Deterrence*, 94–100.
33. See Jonathan G. Utley, "Diplomacy in a Democracy: The United States and Japan, 1937–1941," *World Affairs* 139, no. 2 (Fall 1976): 130–140.
34. See Donald J. Friedman, *The Road from Isolation: The Campaign of the American Committee for Non-Participation in Japanese Aggression, 1938–1941* (Cambridge, MA: Harvard University Press, 1968).

35. Utley, "Diplomacy and Democracy," 132.
36. Quoted in Langer and Gleason, *The Undeclared War*, 654.
37. See Worth, *No Choice but War*, 130–133.
38. Quoted in Nobutake Ike, ed. and trans., *Japan's Decision for War: Records of the 1941 Policy Conferences* (Palo Alto, CA: Stanford University Press, 1967), 147–148.
39. Quoted in ibid., 238.
40. Barnhart, *Japan Prepares for Total War*, 263.
41. Quoted in Ike, *Japan's Decision for War*, 282.
42. Quoted in ibid., 283.
43. Quoted in ibid., 229–230.
44. Worth, *No Choice but War*, 129.
45. Wohlstetter, *Pearl Harbor: Warning and Decision*, 353.
46. Akira Iriye, *Power and Culture: The Japanese-American War, 1941–1945* (Cambridge, MA: Harvard University Press, 1981), 28.
47. Ian Kershaw, *Fateful Choices: Ten Decisions that Changed the World, 1940–1941* (New York: Penguin, 2008), 380.
48. Quoted in Asada, *From Mahan to Pearl Harbor*, 267.
49. George H. E. Smith, "Why Japan Chose to Fight," *Current History* 1, no. 6 (February 1942): 506.
50. Evans and Peattie, *Kaigun*, 410.
51. Ibid., 453.
52. See Barnhart, *Japan Prepares for Total War*, 162; and Morley, *Japan's Road to the Pacific War*, 120–121.
53. Feis, *The Road to Pearl Harbor*, 191.
54. Evans and Peattie, *Kaigun*, 453.
55. Margaret Lamb and Nicholas Tarling, *From Versailles to Pearl Harbor: The Origins of the Second World War in Europe and Asia* (New York: Palgrave, 2001), 7.
56. Louis Morton, "The Japanese Decision for War," *U.S. Naval Institute Proceedings* 80, no. 12 (December 1954): 1334.
57. *Hearings on the Pearl Harbor Attack*, Pt. 11, 5421–5422. For an assessment of allegations that the Roosevelt administration deliberately attempted to maneuver Japan into attacking the United States, see Richard N. Current, "How Stimson Meant to 'Maneuver' the Japanese," *Mississippi Valley Historical Review* 40, no. 1 (June 1953): 67–74.
58. *Judgment of the International Military Tribunal of the Far East* (Tokyo, November 1948), 990, 993. http://www.ibiblio.org/hyperwar/PTO/IMTFE/index.html.

Chapter 4: Japanese Assumptions and Decision Making

1. Pyle, *Japan Rising*, 75.
2. Dower, *War Without Mercy*, 278.

3. Bess, *Choices Under Fire*, 30.
4. For an early assessment of Japanese exploitation of the Monroe Doctrine analogy, see George H. Blakeslee, "The Japanese Monroe Doctrine," *Foreign Affairs* 11, no. 4 (July 1933): 671–681.
5. Dower, *War Without Mercy*, 279.
6. Ike, *Japan's Decision for War*, xxv.
7. Barnhart, *Japan Prepares for Total War*, 167.
8. Morley and Titus, *Japan's Road to the Pacific War*, 121.
9. Butow, *Tojo and the Coming of the War*, 204.
10. Barnhart, *Japan Prepares for Total War*, 167.
11. Quoted in Appendix 2, "Conclusions Reached After Study of 'The Outline for the Execution of the Empire's National Policy' at the Liaison Conference from 23 to 30 October 1941," *Political Strategy Prior to the Outbreak of War, Part IV*, Japan Operational Monograph No. 150 (Washington, DC: Department of the Army, July 1952): 84. http://ibiblio.org/pha/monos/150/index.html.
12. Barnhart, "Japanese Intelligence before the Second World War," in *Knowing One's Enemies*, ed. May, 144.
13. Quoted in B. Mitchell Simpson III, ed., *The Development of Naval Thought: Essays by Herbert Rosinski* (Newport, RI: Naval War College Press, 1977), 106, italics in the original.
14. Ike, *Japan's Decision for War*, 175.
15. Spencer Tucker, ed., *Encyclopedia of World War II: A Political, Social, and Military History* (Santa Barbara, CA: ABC-Clio, 2005), 1541.
16. H. P. Willmott, *Empires in the Balance: Japanese and Allied Pacific Strategies to April 1942* (Annapolis, MD: Naval Institute Press, 1982), 61.
17. Quoted in Asada, *From Mahan to Pearl Harbor*, 183.
18. Compiled from data appearing in Mark Harrison, "The Economics of World War II: An Overview," in *The Economics of World War II: Six Great Powers in International Comparison*, ed. Mark Harrison (New York: Cambridge University Press, 1998), 15–16. Figures exclude landing craft, torpedo boats, and auxiliary vessels.
19. Quoted in Ike, *Japan's Decision for War*, 225.
20. Compiled from data appearing in Harrison, "The Economics of World War II," *The Economics of World War II*, 15–16.
21. Compiled from figures appearing in Willmott, *Empires in the Balance*, 116.
22. Quoted in Morley, *Japan's Road to the Pacific War*, 288.
23. Quoted in Ike, *Japan's Decision for War*, 139.
24. See Dennis Showalter, "Storm over the Pacific: Japan's Road to Empire and War," in *The Pacific War Companion: From Pearl Harbor to Hiroshima*, ed. Daniel Marston (New York: Osprey, 2005), 16–29.
25. Gray, *War, Peace and International Relations*, 180.

26. Quoted in Ike, *Japan's Decision for War*, 153.
27. Quoted in ibid., 207.
28. Quoted in Morley, *Japan's Road to the Pacific War*, 274.
29. Adrian R. Lewis, *The American Culture of War: The History of U.S. Military Force from World War II to Operation Iraqi Freedom* (New York: Routledge, 2007), 59, italics in the original.
30. Bess, *Choices Under Fire*, 53–54.
31. Quoted in Prange, *Pearl Harbor*, 517.
32. Grew, *Ten Years in Japan*, 301–302.
33. H. P. Willmott, "After Midway: Japanese Naval Strategy 1942–1945," in *The Pacific War Companion*, ed. Marston, 178.
34. Quoted in Asada, *From Mahan to Pearl Harbor*, 292.
35. John W. Dower, *War without Mercy: Race and Power in the Pacific War* (New York: Pantheon Books, 1986), 260.
36. Saburo Ienaga, *The Pacific War: World War II and the Japanese, 1931–1945* (New York: Pantheon Books, 1978), 49.
37. John A. Lynn, *Battle: A History of Combat and Culture* (Boulder, CO: Westview Press), 237.
38. Coox, *Nomohan*, 1082.
39. Richard K. Betts, *Surprise Attack: Lessons for Defense Planning* (Washington, DC: Brookings Institution, 1982), 134.
40. Scott D. Sagan, "The Origins of the Pacific War," in *The Origin and Prevention of Major Wars*, eds. Robert I. Rotberg and Theodore K. Rabb (New York: Cambridge University Press, 1989), 324.
41. Langer and Gleason, *The Undeclared War*, 662.
42. Yale Candee Maxon, *Control of Japanese Foreign Policy: A Study of Civil-Military Rivalry 1930–1945* (Berkeley: University of California Press, 1957), 8.
43. Kase, *Journey to the* Missouri, 21.
44. Goldstein and Dillon, *The Pacific War Papers*, 113.
45. Joseph W. Ballantine, "Mukden to Pearl Harbor: The Foreign Policies of Japan," *Foreign Affairs* 27, no. 4 (July 1949): 653.
46. Edward J. Drea, *Japan's Imperial Army: Its Rise and Fall, 1853–1945* (Lawrence: University Press of Kansas, 2009), 127.
47. Akira Fujiwara, "The Role of the Japanese Army," in *Pearl Harbor as History: Japanese-American Relations 1931–1941*, eds. Dorothy Borg and Shumpei Okamoto (New York: Columbia University Press, 1973), 190.
48. United States Strategic Bombing Survey, *The Effects of Strategic Bombing on Japanese Morale*, Reports, Pacific War, no. 14. (Washington, DC: U.S. Government Printing Office, 1947), 139–141.
49. Maxon, *Control of Japanese Foreign Policy*, 120.
50. Ballantine, "Mukden to Pearl Harbor," 651.

51. Quoted in *Pearl Harbor Investigation Report*, 25.
52. Ike, *Japan's Decision for War*, xv.
53. Maxon, *Control of Japanese Foreign Policy*, 158.
54. Ike, *Japan's Decision for War*, xv–xvii.
55. Noriko Kawamura, "Emperor Hirohito and Japan's Decision to Go to War with the United States: Reexamined," *Diplomatic History* (January 2007), 79.
56. Kazuo Yagami, *Konoe Fumimaro and the Failure of Peace in Japan, 1937–1941* (Jefferson, NC: McFarland and Company, 2006), 28.
57. Maxon, *Control of Japanese Foreign Policy*, 150.
58. Ike, *Japan's Decision for War*, xxiv–xxvi.
59. Jack Snyder, *Myths of Empire: Domestic Politics and International Ambition* (Ithaca, NY: Cornell University Press, 1991), 133.
60. Sadao Asada, "The Japanese Navy and the United States," in *Pearl Harbor as History*, eds. Borg and Okamoto, 249.
61. Akira Fujiwara, "The Role of the Japanese Army," 189–195; and Edward J. Drea, *In the Service of the Emperor: Essays on the Imperial Japanese Army* (Lincoln: University of Nebraska Press, 1998), 26, 32.
62. Akira, "The Role of the Japanese Army," 195.
63. Drea, *In the Service of the Emperor*, 43, 45; and Gordon Daniels, "Japan," in *The Oxford Companion to World War II*, ed. Dear, 622.
64. Drea, *Japan's Imperial Army*, 221.
65. Ibid., 242.
66. See Ike, *Japan's Decision for War*, 77–90.
67. Quoted in ibid., 86.
68. Ken Kotani, *Japanese Intelligence in World War I* (New York: Osprey, 209), 148–149.
69. Quoted in Ike, *Japan's Decision for War*, 78, emphasis added.
70. Langer and Gleason, *The Undeclared War*, 636.
71. See Ike, *Japan's Decision for War*, 138–147.
72. Ibid., 152.
73. Ibid.
74. Compiled from Bix, *Hirohito*, 411–412; Butow, *Tojo*, 254–255; and Prange, *At Dawn We Slept*, 208–209. Also see Ike, *Japan's Decision for War*, 133–134.
75. Ike, *Japan's Decision for War*, 202–204.
76. Ibid., 210.
77. Ibid., 212–213.
78. Ibid., 214.
79. Ibid., 238–239.
80. See John Mueller, "Pearl Harbor: Military Inconvenience, Political Disaster," *International Security* 16, no. 3 (Winter 1991–1992): 175–182.
81. Prange, *At Dawn We Slept*, 550. World War II historian Thomas A.

Hughes disagrees. Hughes contends that Nagumo's six aircraft carriers lacked the necessary aircraft and ordnance to attack the U.S Pacific Fleet *and* destroy Pearl Harbor as a port facility and logistical support base. The exception was the mammoth oil storage facility whose above-ground tanks contained 4.5 million barrels of oil. (Conversation with the author, November 3, 2008.)

82. Quoted in Prange, *Pearl Harbor*, 505.
83. See Prange, *At Dawn We Slept*, 29–33, 182–185, 224–231, 297–298.
84. Quoted in Agawa, *The Reluctant Admiral*, 229.
85. Mueller, "Pearl Harbor," 191–194.
86. Black, *Franklin Delano Roosevelt*, 691.
87. Evans and Peattie, *Kaigun*, 493.
88. Ibid., 488, 489.
89. Nish, *Japanese Foreign Policy*, 151.
90. Akira Iriye, *The Origins of the Second World War in Asia and the Pacific* (London: Longman Group, 1987), 75.
91. Evans and Peattie, *Kaigun*, 515, 516, italics in the original.

Chapter 5: Failed Deterrence

1. H. W. Brands, *Traitor to His Class*, 612.
2. See Robert J. Quinlan, "The United States Fleet: Diplomacy, Strategy and the Allocation of Ships (1940–1941)," in *American Civil-Military Decisions: A Book of Case Studies*, ed. Harold Stein (Tuscaloosa: University of Alabama Press, 1963), 153–198.
3. Quoted in Herzog, *Closing the Open Door*, 62.
4. Quoted in Agawa, *The Reluctant Admiral*, 227–228 (emphasis in original).
5. Morton, *Strategy and Command*, 85.
6. Memorandum of conversation between President Roosevelt and Assistant Secretary of State Sayre, November 16, 1936, quoted in James H. Herzog, *Closing the Open Door: American-Japanese Diplomatic Negotiations, 1936–1941* (Annapolis, MD: Naval Institute Press, 1973), 7.
7. Morton, *Strategy and Command*, 100–101.
8. See Daniel F. Harrington, "A Careless Hope: American Air Power and Japan, 1941," *Pacific Historical Review* 48, no. 2 (May 1979): 217–238; and Russell F. Weigley, "The Role of the War Department and the Army," in *Pearl Harbor as History*, eds. Borg and Okamoto, 165–195.
9. Quoted in Feis, *The Road to Pearl Harbor*, 300.
10. Harrington, "A Careless Hope," 226–230.
11. Morton, *Strategy and Command*, 98.
12. Ibid., 99.

13. Edwin Layton with Roger Pineau and John Costello, *"And I Was There": Pearl Harbor and Midway—Breaking the Secrets* (Old Saybrook, CT: Konecky and Konecky, 1985), 133.
14. Bruce M. Russett, *No Clear and Present Danger: A Skeptical View of U.S. Entry Into World War II* (New York: Harper and Row, 1972), 50.
15. Herzog, *Closing the Open Door*, 100–101.
16. Quoted in ibid., 191.
17. Cited in Robert E. Sherwood, *Roosevelt and Hopkins: An Intimate History* (New York: Enigma Books, 2008 [1948]), 277, emphasis added.
18. Barnhart, *Japan Prepares for Total War*, 271.
19. Hull, *Memoirs*, 983.
20. Letter from Grew to Roosevelt, December 14, 1940, *Hearings on the Pearl Harbor Attack*, Part 2, 631.
21. *Hearings on the Pearl Harbor Attack*, Part 2, 583.
22. Frederick W. Marks III, "The Origin of FDR's Promise to Support Britain Militarily in the Far East—A New Look," *Pacific Historical Review* 53, no. 4 (November 1984): 147. Also see James MacGregor Burns, *Roosevelt: Soldier of Freedom* (New York: Harcourt, 1970), 159–161; and Robert Dallek, *Franklin D. Roosevelt and American Foreign Policy, 1932–1945* (New York: Oxford University Press, 1979), 308–311.
23. Sherwood, *Roosevelt and Hopkins*, 340–341.
24. Ibid., 336–337.
25. Quoted in ibid., 335, 336.
26. Morton, *Strategy and Command*, 125.
27. Quoted in Morley, *Japan's Road to the Pacific War*, 340.
28. David Klein and Hilary Conroy, "Churchill, Roosevelt, and the China Question in Pre-Pearl Harbor Diplomacy," in *Pearl Harbor Reexamined*, eds. Conroy and Wray, 130–131.
29. Worth, *No Choice but War*, x, 100.
30. Russett, *No Clear and Present Danger*, 45, 47.
31. John Toland, *The Rising Sun: The Decline and Fall of the Japanese Empire, 1936–1945* (New York: Random House, 1970), 146, 147.
32. See Prange, *At Dawn We Slept*, 358–359, 369.
33. Herring, *From Colony to Superpower*, 536.
34. Schroeder, *The Axis Alliance*, 177.
35. Quoted in Langer and Gleason, *The Undeclared War*.
36. Quoted verbatim in ibid., 872, italics in the original.
37. Quoted in *Pearl Harbor Attack Investigation Report*, 36.
38. Ibid.
39. Schroeder, *The Axis Alliance*, 85.
40. Langer and Gleason, *The Undeclared War*, 721.
41. Schroeder, *The Axis Alliance*, 199.

42. Mark A. Stoler, "The Roosevelt Foreign Policy: Flawed, But Superior to the Competition," in Justus D. Doenecke and Mark A. Stoler, *Debating Franklin D. Roosevelt's Foreign Policies, 1933–1945* (New York: Rowman & Littlefield, 2005), 144–145.
43. Schroeder, 181, 202.
44. Ibid., 182.
45. Ibid., 201.
46. Ibid., 215.

Chapter 6: Was the Pacific War Inevitable?

1. Andrew Gordon, *A Modern History of Japan: From Tokugawa Times to the Present* (New York: Harvard University Press, 2003), 209.
2. Bess, *Choices Under Fire*, 56.
3. Pyle, *Japan Rising*, 62.
4. Ibid., 98.
5. Ibid., 109.
6. See the author's "Operational Brilliance, Strategic Incompetence: The Military Reformers and the German Model," *Parameters* 16, no. 3 (Autumn 1986).
7. Worth, *No Choice but War*, 219.
8. See Lu, *From the Marco Polo Bridge to Pearl Harbor*, 226–227.

Chapter 7: The Enduring Lessons of 1941

1. Thucydides, in Strassler, *The Landmark Thucydides*, 16 (emphasis added).
2. Prange, *At Dawn We Slept*, 752.
3. Maxon, *Control of Japanese Foreign Policy*, 29.
4. Ibid., 173.
5. Dennis Showalter, "Foreword," in James S. Corum, *Bad Strategies: How Major Powers Failed in Counterinsurgency* (Minneapolis, MN: Zenith Press, 2008), 8.
6. Colin S. Gray, "The American Way of War: Critique and Implications," in *Rethinking the Principles of War*, ed. Anthony D. Mc Ivor (Annapolis, MD: Naval Institute Press, 2005), 29.
7. Pyle, *Japan Rising*, 193.
8. *Mao Tse-tung on Guerrilla Warfare*, trans. by Samuel B. Griffith (New York: Praeger Publishers, 1961), 55, 56.
9. See Ivan Arreguin-Toft, *How the Weak Win Wars: A Theory of Asymmetric Conflict* (New York: Cambridge University Press, 2005); Andrew Mack, "Why Big Nations Lose Small Wars: The Politics of Asymmetric Conflict," *World Politics* 27, no. 2 (1975): 175–200; and Gil Merom, *How Democracies Lose Small Wars: State, Society, and the*

Failures of France in Algeria, Israel in Lebanon, and the United States in Vietnam (New York: Cambridge University Press, 2003).

10. See the author's "The Limits and Temptations of America's Conventional Military Primacy," *Survival* 47, no. 1 (Spring 2005): 33–50.

11. See the author's "Why the Bush Administration Invaded Iraq: Making Strategy after 9/11," *Strategic Studies Quarterly* 2, no. 2 (Summer 2008): 63–92. An expanded assessment of the subject is available in *Wanting War: Why the Bush Administration Invaded Iraq* (Washington, DC: Potomac Books, 2010).

12. Steven Simon, "The Price of the Surge: How U.S. Strategy is Hastening Iraq's Demise," *Foreign Affairs* 87, no. 3 (May/June 2008): 61.

13. See Akbar Ganji, "The Latter-Day Sultan: Power and Politics in Iran," *Foreign Affairs* 87, no. 6 (November/December 2008): 45–66; and Thomas Powers, "Iran: The Threat," *New York Review of Books*, July 17, 2008. Also see the author's "Retiring Hitler and 'Appeasement' from the National Security Debate," *Parameters* 38, no. 2 (Summer 2008): esp. 96–98.

14. See James Fallows, "Will Iran Be Next?" *Atlantic Monthly* 294, no. 5 (December 2004); Whitney Raas and Austin Long, "Osirak Redux? Assessing Israeli Capabilities to Destroy Iranian Nuclear Facilities," *International Security* 31, no. 4 (Spring 2007): 7–43; and Justin Logan, *The Bottom Line on Iran: The Costs and Benefits of Preventive War versus Deterrence*, Policy Analysis Paper 583 (Washington, DC: Cato Institute, December 4, 2006).

15. Stephen Kinzer, "The Folly of Attacking Iran," in *All the Shah's Men: An American Coup and the Roots of Middle East Terror*, ed. Stephen Kinzer (New York: John Wiley and Sons, 2008), xii.

BIBLIOGRAPHY

Acheson, Dean. *Present at the Creation: My Years in the State Department.* New York: W. W. Norton, 1969.

Adams, Frederick C. "The Road to Pearl Harbor: A Reexamination of American Far Eastern Policy, July 1937–December 1938." *Journal of American History* 58, no.1 (June 1971): 73–92.

Agawa, Hiroyuki. *The Reluctant Admiral: Yamamoto and the Imperial Navy.* Translated by John Bester. Tokyo: Kondansha International, 1979.

Anderson, Irvine H., Jr. "The 1941 *De Facto* Embargo on Oil to Japan: A Bureaucratic Reflex." *Pacific Historical Review* 44, no. 2 (May 1975): 201–231.

Aron, Raymond. *Peace and War: A Theory of International Politics.* New Brunswick, NJ: Transaction Publishers, 2003.

Arreguin-Toft, Ivan. *How the Weak Win Wars: A Theory of Asymmetric Conflict.* New York: Cambridge University Press, 2005.

Asada, Sadao. *From Mahan to Pearl Harbor: The Imperial Japanese Navy and the United States.* Annapolis, MD: Naval Institute Press, 2006.

Ballantine, Joseph W. "Mukden to Pearl Harbor: The Foreign Policies of Japan." *Foreign Affairs* 27, no. 4 (July 1949): 651–664.

Barnhart, Michael A. *Japan Prepares for Total War: The Search for Economic Security, 1919–1941.* Ithaca, NY: Cornell University Press, 1987.

———. "Japanese Intelligence before the Second World War: 'Best Case' Analysis." In *Knowing One's Enemies: Intelligence Assessment before the Two World Wars,* edited by Ernest R. May, 424–455. Princeton, NJ: Princeton University Press, 1986.

———. "The Origins of the Second World War in Asia and the Pacific: Synthesis Impossible?" *Diplomatic History* 20, no. 2 (Spring 1996): 241–260.

Bell, P. M. H. "Origins of the War." In *The Oxford Companion to World War II*, edited by I. C. B. Dear, 840–846. New York: Oxford University Press, 1995.

Ben-Zvi, Abraham. *The Illusion of Deterrence: The Roosevelt Presidency and the Origins of the Pacific War*. Boulder, CO: Westview Press, 1987.

Bess, Michael. *Choices Under Fire: Moral Dimensions of World War II*. New York: Vintage Books, 2006.

Best, Anthony, "Imperial Japan." In *The Origins of World War II: The Debate Continues*, edited by Robert Boyce and Joseph A. Mailolo, 52–69. New York: Palgrave Macmillan, 2003.

Betts, Richard K. *Surprise Attack: Lessons for Defense Planning*. Washington, DC: Brookings Institution, 1982.

Bix, Herbert P. *Hirohito and the Making of Modern Japan*. New York: Harper Collins, 2000.

Black, Conrad. *Franklin Delano Roosevelt: Champion of Freedom*. New York: Public Affairs, 2003.

Blakeslee, George H. "The Japanese Monroe Doctrine." *Foreign Affairs* 11, no. 4 (July 1933): 671–681.

Blum, John Morton. *From the Morgenthau Diaries*. Vol. 2, *Years of Urgency: 1938–1941*. Boston: Houghton Mifflin, 1965.

Borg, Dorothy, and Shumpei Okamoto, eds. *Pearl Harbor as History: Japanese-American Relations, 1931–1941*. New York: Columbia University Press, 1973.

Brands, H. C. *Traitor to His Class: The Privileged Life and Radical Presidency of Franklin Delano Roosevelt*. New York: Doubleday, 2008.

Breen, John, ed. *Yasukuni: The War Dead and the Struggle for Japan's Past*. Singapore: Horizon Books, 2007.

Burns, James MacGregor. *Roosevelt: The Soldier of Freedom 1940–1945*. New York: Harcourt, 1970.

Butow, Robert J. C. *Tojo and the Coming of the War*. Princeton, NJ: Princeton University Press, 1961.

Chapman, John. "The Imperial Japanese Navy and the North-South Dilemma." In *Barbarossa: The Axis and the Allies*, John Erickson and David Dilks, 150–206. Edinburgh: Edinburgh University Press, 1994.

Churchill, Winston S. *The War Speeches of Winston S. Churchill, 1939–1945*. Compiled by Charles Ead. 3 vols. London: Cassell and Company, 1952.

Conroy, Hilary, and Harry Wray, eds. *Pearl Harbor Reexamined: Prologue to the Pacific War*. Honolulu: University of Hawaii Press, 1990.

Coox, Alvin D. *Nomonhan: Japan against Russia, 1939*. Palo Alto, CA: Stanford University Press, 1985.

Costello, John. *The Pacific War 1941–1945*. New York: Rawson, Wade, 1981.

Crowley, James B. *Japan's Quest for Autonomy: National Security and Foreign Policy, 1930–1938*. Princeton, NJ: Princeton University Press, 1966.

Crozier, Andrew J. *The Causes of the Second World War*. Malden, MA: Blackwell, 1997.

Current, Richard N. "How Stimson Meant to 'Maneuver' the Japanese." *Mississippi Valley Historical Review* 40, no. 1 (June 1953): 67–74.

Dallek, Robert. *Franklin Roosevelt and American Foreign Policy, 1932–1945*. New York: Oxford University Press, 1979.

Daniels, Gordon, "Japan." In *The Oxford Companion to World War II*, edited by I. C. B. Dear, 605–633. New York: Oxford University Press, 1995.

Daniels, Roger. *The Politics of Prejudice: The Anti-Japanese Movement in California and the Struggle for Japanese Exclusion*. Berkeley: University of California Press, 1977.

D'Este, Carlo. *Warlord: A Life of Winston Churchill at War*. New York: HarperCollins, 2008.

Divine, Robert A. *The Reluctant Belligerent: American Entry into World War II*. New York: John Wiley and Sons, 1965.

Doenecke, Justus D., and Mark A. Stoler. *Debating Franklin D. Roosevelt's Foreign Policies, 1933–1945*. New York: Rowman & Littlefield, 2005.

Dower, John W. *War Without Mercy: Race and Power in the Pacific War*. New York: Pantheon Books, 1986.

Doyle, Michael K. "The United States Navy—Strategy and Far Eastern Foreign Policy, 1931–1941." *Naval War College Review* 30, no. 3 (Winter 1977): 52–59.

Drea, Edward J. *In the Service of the Emperor: Essays on the Imperial Japanese Army*. Lincoln: University of Nebraska Press, 1998.

———. *Japan's Imperial Army: Its Rise and Fall, 1853–1945*. Lawrence: University Press of Kansas, 2009.

Esthus, Raymond A. "President Roosevelt's Commitment to Britain to Intervene in a Pacific War." *Pacific Historical Review* 50, no. 1 (June 1963): 28–38.

Evans, David C., and Mark R. Peattie. *Kaigun: Strategy, Tactics, and Technology in the Imperial Japanese Navy, 1887–1941*. Annapolis, MD: Naval Institute Press, 1997.

Fallows, James. "Will Iran Be Next?" *Atlantic Monthly* 294, no. 5 (December 2004): 99–110.

Feis, Herbert. *The Road to Pearl Harbor: The Coming of the War Between the United States and Japan*. Princeton, NJ: Princeton University Press, 1950.

Friedman, Donald J. *The Road from Isolation: The Campaign of the American Committee for Non-Participation in Japanese Aggression, 1938–1941*. Cambridge, MA: Harvard University Press, 1968.

Fujiwara, Akira. "The Role of the Japanese Army." In *Pearl Harbor as History: Japanese-American Relations 1931–1941*, edited by Dorothy Borg and Shumpei Okamoto, 189–195. New York: Columbia University Press, 1973.

Ganji, Akbar. "The Latter-Day Sultan: Power and Politics in Iran." *Foreign Affairs* 87, no. 6 (November/December 2008): 45–66.

Goldstein, Donald M., and Katherine V. Dillon, eds. *The Pacific War Papers: Japanese Documents of World War II*. Washington, DC: Potomac Books, 2004.

Gordon, Andrew. *A History of Modern Japan: From Tokugawa Times to the Present*. New York: Oxford University Press, 2003.

Gray, Colin S. "The American Way of War: Critique and Implications." In *Rethinking the Principles of War*, edited by Anthony D. McIvor, 13–40. Annapolis, MD: Naval Institute Press, 2005.

———. *War, Peace and International Relations: An Introduction to Strategic History*. New York: Routledge, 2007.

Grew, Joseph C. *Ten Years in Japan: A Contemporary Record Drawn from the Diaries and Private and Official Papers of Joseph C. Grew*. New York: Simon and Schuster, 1944.

———. *Turbulent Era: A Diplomatic Record of Forty Years, 1904–1945*. Edited by Walter Johnson. 2 vols. Boston: Houghton Mifflin, 1952.

Gruhl, Werner. *Imperial Japan's World War II, 1931–1945*. New Brunswick, NJ: Transaction Publishers, 2007.

Haight, John McVickar, Jr. "Franklin D. Roosevelt and a Naval Quarantine of Japan." *Pacific Historical Review* 40, no. 2 (May 1971): 203–226.

Harries, Meirion, and Susie Harries. *Soldiers of the Sun: The Rise and Fall of the Imperial Japanese Army*. New York: Random House, 1991.

Harrington, Daniel F. "A Careless Hope: American Air Power and Japan, 1941." *Pacific Historical Review* 48, no. 2 (May 1979): 217–238.

Harrison, Mark, ed. *The Economics of World War II: Six Great Powers in International Comparison*. New York: Cambridge University Press, 1998.

Hart, B. H. Liddell. *Strategy*. 2nd edition. New York: Frederick A. Praeger, 1967.

Hearings before the Joint Committee on the Investigation of the Pearl Harbor Attack. 79th Cong., 1st sess. Part 2. Washington, DC: U.S. Government Printing Office, 1946.

Heinrichs, Waldo. "The Russian Factor and Japanese-American Relations, 1941." In *Pearl Harbor Reexamined: Prologue to the Pacific War*, edited by Hilary Conroy and Harry Wray, 163–177. Honolulu: University of Hawaii Press, 1990.

———. *Threshold of War: Franklin D. Roosevelt and American Entry into World War II*. New York: Oxford University Press, 1988.

Herring, George. *From Colony to Superpower: U.S. Foreign Relations Since 1776*. New York: Oxford University Press, 2008.

Herzog, James H. *Closing the Open Door: American-Japanese Diplomatic Relations 1936–1941*. Annapolis, MD: Naval Institute Press, 1973.

———. "Influence of the United States Navy in the Embargo of Oil to Japan, 1940–1941." *Pacific Historical Review* 35, no. 3 (August 1966): 317–328.

Hosoya, Chihiro. "Twenty-Five Years after Pearl Harbor: A New Look at Japan's Decision for War." In *Imperial Japan: A Reassessment*, compiled by Grant K. Goodman, 52–64. New York: East Asian Institute, Columbia University, 1967.

Hull, Cordell. *The Memoirs of Cordell Hull*. 2 vols. New York: Macmillan, 1948.

Ickes, Harold L. *The Secret Diary of Harold L. Ickes*. 3 vols. New York: Simon and Schuster, 1954.

Ike, Nobutaka, ed. *Japan's Decision for War: Records of the 1941 Policy Conferences*. Palo Alto, CA: Stanford University Press, 1967.

Ienaga, Saburo. *The Pacific War: World War II and the Japanese, 1931–1945*. New York: Pantheon Books, 1978.

Iriye, Akira. *The Origins of the Second World War in Asia and the Pacific*. London: Longman Group, 1987.

———. *Pearl Harbor and the Coming of the Pacific War: A Brief History with Documents and Essays*. Boston: Bedford/St. Martin's, 1999.

———. *Power and Culture: The Japanese-American War, 1941–1945*. Cambridge, MA: Harvard University Press, 1981.

Ishizu, Tomoyuki, and Raymond Callahan. "The Rising Sun Strikes: The Japanese Invasions." In *The Pacific War Companion: From Pearl Harbor to Hiroshima*, edited by Daniel Marston, 45–58. New York: Osprey, 2005.

Judgment of the International Military Tribunal of the Far East. Tokyo, November 1948. http://www.ibiblio.org/hyperwar/PTO/IMTFE/IMTFE-7.html.

Kahn, David. "United States Views of Germany and Japan in 1941." In *Knowing One's Enemies: Intelligence Before the Two World Wars*, Ernest R. May, 476–502. Princeton, NJ: Princeton University Press, 1986.

Kase, Toshikazu. *Journey to the Missouri*. New Haven, CT: Yale University Press, 1950.

Kato, Masuo. *The Lost War: A Japanese Reporter's Inside Story*. New York: Alfred A. Knopf, 1946.

Kawamura, Noriko. "Emperor Hirohito and Japan's Decision to Go to War with the United States: Reexamined." *Diplomatic History* 31, no. 1 (January 2007): 51–79.

Kennan, George F. *American Diplomacy, 1900–1950*. Chicago: University of Chicago Press, 1951.

Kershaw, Ian. *Fateful Choices: Ten Decisions that Changed the World, 1940–1941*. New York: Penguin, 2007.

Kinzer, Stephen. "The Folly of Attacking Iran." In *All the Shah's Men: An American Coup and the Roots of Middle East Terror*. New York: John Wiley and Sons, 2008.

Klein, David, and Hilary Conroy. "Churchill, Roosevelt, and the China Question in Pre-Pearl Harbor Diplomacy." In *Pearl Harbor Reexamined: Prologue to the Pacific War*, edited by Hilary Conroy and Harry Wray. Honolulu: University of Hawaii Press, 1990.

Komatsu, Keiichiro. *Origins of the Pacific War and the Importance of "Magic."* New York: St. Martin's Press, 1999.

Kotani, Ken. *Japanese Intelligence in World War II*. New York: Osprey, 2009.

———. "Pearl Harbor: Japanese Planning and Command Structure." In *The Pacific War Companion: From Pearl Harbor to Hiroshima*, edited by Daniel Marston, 30–44. New York: Osprey, 2005.

LaFeber, Walter. *The Clash: U.S.-Japanese Relations Throughout History*. New York: W. W. Norton, 1997.

Lamb, Margaret, and Nicholas Tarling. *From Versailles to Pearl Harbor: The Origins of the Second World War in Europe and Asia*. New York: Palgrave, 2001.

Langer, William L., and S. Everett Gleason. *The Undeclared War, 1940–1941: The World Crisis and American Foreign Policy*. New York: Harper and Brothers, 1953.

Layton, Edwin T., with Roger Pineau and John Costello. *"And I Was There": Pearl Harbor and Midway—Breaking the Secrets*. Old Saybrook, CT: Konecky and Konecky, 1985.

Lewis, Adrian R. *The American Culture of War: The History of U.S. Military Force from World War II to Operation Iraqi Freedom*. New York: Routledge, 2007.

Libby, Justin H. "Rendezvous with Disaster." *World Affairs* 158, no. 2 (Winter 1996): 137–147.

Lind, Jennifer. "The Perils of Apology: What Japan Shouldn't Learn from Germany." *Foreign Affairs* 88, no. 3 (May/June 2009): 132–146.

Logan, Justin. *The Bottom Line on Iran: The Costs and Benefits of Preventive War versus Deterrence*. Policy Analysis Paper 583. Washington, DC: Cato Institute, December 4, 2006.

Lu, David J. *From the Marco Polo Bridge to Pearl Harbor: Japan's Entry into World War II*. Washington, DC: Public Affairs Press, 1961.

Luttwak, Edward N. *Strategy: The Logic of War and Peace*. Cambridge, MA: Belknap Press, 1987.

Lynn, John A. *Battle: A History of Combat and Culture*. Boulder, CO: Westview Press, 2003.

Mack, Andrew. "Why Big Nations Lose Small Wars: The Politics of Asymmetric Conflict." *World Politics* 27, no. 2 (1975): 175–200.

Macmillan, Margaret. *Paris 1919: Six Months that Changed the World*. New York: Random House, 2001.

Mao Tse-tung on Guerrilla Warfare. Translated by Samuel B. Griffith. New York: Praeger Publishers, 1961.

Marks, Frederick W., III. "The Origins of FDR's Promise to Support Britain Militarily in the Far East—A New Look." *Pacific Historical Review* 53, no. 4 (November 1984): 447–462.

Marshall, Jonathan. *To Have and Have Not: Southeast Asian Raw Materials and the Origins of the Pacific War*. Berkeley: University of California Press, 1995.

Masland, John W. "Missionary Influence Upon American Far Eastern Policy." *Pacific Historical Review* 10, no. 3 (September 1941): 279–296.

Mauch, Peter. "Revisiting Nomura's Diplomacy: Ambassador Nomura's Role in the Japanese-American Negotiations, 1941." *Diplomatic History* 28, no. 3 (June 2004): 353–383.

Maxon, Yale Candee. *Control of Japanese Foreign Policy: A Study of Civil-Military Rivalry, 1930–1945*. Berkeley: University of California Press, 1957.

Merom, Gil. *How Democracies Lose Small Wars: State, Society, and the Failures of France in Algeria, Israel in Lebanon, and the United States in Vietnam*. New York: Cambridge University Press, 2003.

Miller, Edward S. *Bankrupting the Enemy: The U.S. Financial Siege of Japan before Pearl Harbor*. Annapolis, MD: Naval Institute Press, 2007.

Morley, James William, ed., David A. Titus, trans. *Japan's Road to the Pacific War, The Final Confrontation: Japan's Negotiations with the United States, 1941*. New York: Columbia University Press, 1994.

Morton, Louis. "The Japanese Decision for War." *U.S. Naval Institute Proceedings* 80, no. 12 (December 1954): 1325–1335.

———. *The War in the Pacific, Strategy and Command: The First Two Years*. Washington, DC: Center of Military History, U.S. Army, 1962.

Mueller, John. "Pearl Harbor: Military Inconvenience, Political Disaster." *International Security* 16, no. 3 (Winter 1991–1992): 175–182.

Murakami, Sachiko. "Indochina: Unplanned Incursion." In *Pearl Harbor Reexamined: Prologue to the Pacific War*, edited by Hilary Conroy and Harry Wray, 141–149. Honolulu: University of Hawaii Press, 1990.

Neumann, William L. "Franklin D. Roosevelt and Japan, 1913–1933." *Pacific Historical Review* 22, no. 2 (May 1953): 143–153.

Nish, Ian. *Japanese Foreign Policy in the Interwar Period*. New York: Praeger, 2002.

Nomura, Kichisaburo. "Japan's Demand for Naval Equality." *Foreign Affairs* 13, no. 2 (January 1935): 196–203.

———. "Stepping Stones to War." *U.S. Naval Institute Proceedings* 77, no. 9 (September 1951): 927–931.

Onishi, Norimitsu. "Japan Fires General Who Said a U.S. 'Trap' Led to Pearl Harbor." *New York Times*, November 1, 2008.

Pelz, Stephen E. *Race to Pearl Harbor: The Failure of the Second London Naval Conference and the Onset of World War II*. Cambridge, MA: Harvard University Press, 1974.

Powers, Thomas. "Iran: The Threat." *New York Review of Books* 55, no. 12 (July 17, 2008): 9–11.

Prange, Gordon W., with Donald M. Goldstein and Katherine V. Dillon. *At Dawn We Slept: The Untold Story of Pearl Harbor*. New York: McGraw-Hill, 1981.

———. *Pearl Harbor: The Verdict of History*. New York: McGraw-Hill, 1986.

Pyle, Kenneth B. *Japan Rising: The Resurgence of Japanese Power and Purpose*. New York: Public Affairs, 2007.

Quinlan, Robert J. "The United States Fleet: Diplomacy, Strategy and the Allocation of Ships (1940–1941)." In *American Civil-Military Decisions: A Book of Case Studies*, edited by Harold Stein, 163–198. Tuscaloosa: University of Alabama Press, 1963: 163–198.

Raas, Whitney, and Austin Long. "Osirak Redux? Assessing Israeli Capabilities to Destroy Iranian Nuclear Facilities." *International Security* 31, no. 4 (Spring 2007): 7–43.

Record, Jeffrey. *Dark Victory: America's Second War Against Iraq*. Annapolis, MD: Naval Institute Press, 2004.

———. "The Limits and Temptations of America's Conventional Military Primacy." *Survival* 47, no. 1 (Spring 2005): 33–50.

———. "Retiring Hitler and 'Appeasement' from the National Security Debate." *Parameters* 38, no. 2 (Summer 2008): 91–101.

———. "Why the Bush Administration Invaded Iraq: Making Strategy After 9/11." *Strategic Studies Quarterly* 2, no. 2 (Summer 2008): 63–92.

———. *The Wrong War: Why We Lost in Vietnam*. Annapolis, MD: Naval Institute Press, 1998.

Report of the Joint Committee on the Investigation of the Pearl Harbor Attack. 79th Cong., 2nd sess. Washington, DC: U.S. Government Printing Office, 1946.

Reynolds, David. *In Command of History: Churchill Fighting and Writing the Second World War*. New York: Basic Books, 2005.

Russett, Bruce M. *No Clear and Present Danger: A Skeptical View of U.S. Entry into World War*. New York: Harper and Row, 1972.

Sagan, Scott. "The Origins of the Pacific War." In *The Origin and Prevention of Major Wars*, edited by Robert I. Rotberg and Theodore K. Rabb, 323–352. New York: Cambridge University Press, 1989.

Schroeder, Paul W. *The Axis Alliance and Japanese-American Relations.* Ithaca, NY: Cornell University Press, 1958.

Sherwood, Robert E. *Roosevelt and Hopkins: An Intimate History.* New York: Enigma Books, 2008 (1948).

Showalter, Dennis. "Foreword." In *Bad Strategies: How Major Powers Failed in Counterinsurgency,* edited by James S. Corum. Minneapolis, MN: Zenith Press, 2008.

Simpson, B. Mitchell, III. *The Development of Naval Thought: Essays by Herbert Rosinski.* Newport, RI: Naval War College Press, 1977.

———. "Storm over the Pacific: Japan's Road to Empire and War." In *The Pacific War Companion: From Pearl Harbor to Hiroshima,* edited by Daniel Marston, 16–29. New York: Osprey, 2005.

Simon, Steven. "The Price of the Surge: How U.S. Strategy is Hastening Iraq's Demise." *Foreign Affairs* 87, no. 3 (May/June 2008): 57–76.

Smith, George H. E. "Why Japan Chose to Fight." *Current History* 1, no. 6 (February 1942): 501–506.

Smith, Jean Edward. *FDR.* New York: Random House, 2007.

Snyder, Jack. *Myths of Empire: Domestic Politics and International Ambition.* Ithaca, NY: Cornell University Press, 1991.

Stimson, Henry L. *The Far Eastern Crisis — Recollections and Observations.* New York: Harper Brothers, 1936.

———. *On Active Service in Peace and War.* New York: Harper, 1948.

Strassler, Robert, ed. *The Landmark Thucydides: A Comprehensive Guide to the Peloponnesian War.* New York: Free Press, 1996.

Sun, Youli. *China and the Origins of the Pacific War, 1931–1941.* New York: St. Martin's Press, 1993.

Tohmatsu, Haruo, and H. P. Wilmott. *A Gathering Darkness: The Coming of War to the Far East and the Pacific, 1921–1942.* New York: S R Books, 2004.

Toland, John. *The Rising Sun: The Decline and Fall of the Japanese Empire, 1936–1945.* New York: Random House, 1970.

Tucker, Spencer, ed. *Encyclopedia of World War II: A Political, Social, and Military History.* Santa Barbara, CA: ABC-Clio, 2005.

United States Strategic Bombing Survey. *The Effects of Strategic Bombing on Japanese Morale.* Reports, Pacific War, No. 14. Washington, DC: U.S. Government Printing Office, 1947.

U.S. Department of the Army. Office of the Chief of Military History. "Conclusions Reached After Study of 'The Outline for the Execution of the Empire's National Policy' at the Liaison Conference from 23 to 30 October 1941." In *Political Strategy Prior to the Outbreak of War, Part IV.* Washington, DC, July 1952. http://ibiblio.org/pha/monos/150/index.html.

U.S. Department of State. *Foreign Relations of the United States: Japan:*

1931–1941. Vol. 2. Washington, DC: U.S. Government Printing Office, 1943.

Utley, Jonathan G. "Diplomacy in a Democracy: The United States and Japan, 1937–1941." *World Affairs* 139, no. 2 (Fall 1976): 130–140.

———. *Going to War with Japan, 1937–1941.* Knoxville: University of Tennessee Press, 1985.

Van Slyke, Lyman P. "China." In *The Oxford Companion to World War II,* edited by I. C. B. Dear, 210–224. New York: Oxford University Press, 1995.

Willmott, H. P. "After Midway: Japanese Naval Strategy 1942–1945." In *The Pacific War Companion: Pearl Harbor to Hiroshima,* edited by Daniel Marston, 177–191. New York: Osprey, 2005.

———. *Empires in the Balance: Japanese and Allied Pacific Strategies to April 1942.* Annapolis, MD: Naval Institute Press, 1982.

———. *The War with Japan: The Period of Balance, May 1942–October 1943.* Wilmington, DE: Scholarly Resources Books, 2002.

Wohlstetter, Roberta. *Pearl Harbor: Warning and Decision.* Palo Alto, CA: Stanford University Press, 1962.

Wood, James B. *Japanese Military Strategy and the Pacific War: Was Defeat Inevitable?* New York: Rowman & Littlefield, 2007.

Worth, Roland H., Jr. *No Choice but War: The United States Embargo Against Japan and the Eruption of War in the Pacific.* Jefferson, NC: McFarland and Company, 1995.

Yagami, Kazuo. *Konoe Fumimaro and the Failure of Peace in Japan, 1937–1941: A Critical Appraisal of the Three-time Prime Minister.* Jefferson, NC: McFarland and Company, 2006.

INDEX

ABOUT THE AUTHOR

Well-known defense policy critic Jeffrey Record teaches strategy at the U.S. Air Force's Air War College in Montgomery, Alabama. He received his doctorate at the Johns Hopkins School of Advanced International Studies and is the author of eight books and a dozen monographs, including: *Wanting War: Why the Bush Administration Invaded Iraq; Beating Goliath: Why Insurgencies Win; Dark Victory: America's Second War Against Iraq; Making War, Thinking History: Munich, Vietnam, and Presidential Uses of Force from Korea to Kosovo; Hollow Victory: A Contrary View of the Gulf War; The Wrong War: Why We Lost in Vietnam;* and *Bounding the Global War on Terrorism.* Dr. Record has served as a pacification adviser in the Mekong Delta during the Vietnam War, Rockefeller Younger Scholar on the Brookings Institution's Defense Analysis Staff, and Senior Fellow at the Institute for Foreign Policy Analysis, the Hudson Institute, and the BDM International Corporation. He also has extensive Capitol Hill experience, serving as Legislative Assistant for National Security Affairs to senators Sam Nunn and Lloyd Bentsen, and later as a Professional Staff Member of the Senate Armed Services Committee. He lives in Atlanta, Georgia, with his wife, Leigh.